TRAVELLERS

TUNISIA

By
DIANA DARKE

Written and updated by Diana Darke
Additional research by Conor Caffrey

Original photography by Paul Kenward and Ethel Davies
Additional photograph by Conor Caffrey

Editing and page layout by Cambridge Publishing Management Ltd,
Unit 2, Burr Elm Court, Caldecote CB23 7NU
Series Editor: Karen Beaulah

Published by Thomas Cook Publishing
A division of Thomas Cook Tour Operations Ltd
Company Registration No. 1450464 England

PO Box 227, The Thomas Cook Business Park,
Coningsby Road, Peterborough PE3 8SB, United Kingdom
E-mail: books@thomascook.com
www.thomascookpublishing.com
Tel: +44 (0)1733 416477

ISBN: 978-1-84157-794-4

Text © 2007 Thomas Cook Publishing
Maps © 2007 Thomas Cook Publishing
First edition © 2005 Thomas Cook Publishing
Second edition © 2007 Thomas Cook Publishing

Project Editor: Sasha Heseltine
Production/DTP Editor: Steven Collins

Printed and bound in Italy by: Printer Trento.

Front cover credits: © Thomas Cook, © World Pictures, © Thomas Cook
Back cover credits: © Thomas Cook, © Thomas Cook

Contents

KEY TO MAPS

✈ Airport

Ⓜ Metro station

★ Start of walk/drive

736m ▲ Mountain

[i] Information

[5] Road number

Introduction

Tunisia is well known as a package destination but, for those who care to look further than its beach resorts, it offers far more. Beyond the excellent beaches and the rows of comfortable low-rise hotels lies a country of tremendous variety. The north is a landscape of green mountains, rivers and lakes. The south is dominated by arid desert with sporadic green oases and the spectacular dunes of the Sahara's Grand Erg Oriental.

Concealed in the interior are caves, gorges, waterfalls and salt lakes. Tunisia is also dotted with a staggering 250 historic sites, the better known of which are served by luxury hotels as more and more people discover the rich rewards of looking beyond Tunisia's coastline.

Sandwiched between Libya and Algeria, Tunisia walks a tightrope, wishing to maintain good relations with its Maghrebi (Arab North African) neighbours, yet wanting to avoid the pitfalls of their political problems. At the centre of the Mediterranean world, Tunisia has seen a constant passage of armies over the centuries – from Phoenicians, Romans and Vandals to Byzantines, Turks and French – all of whom left their mark and contributed to the cultural melding that is part of Tunisia's fascination and appeal today. In the 20th century, President Habib Bourguiba forged the country's national identity, favouring a pro-Western outlook and introducing many social reforms. More recently, President Ben Ali has continued some of these reforms.

An Arab country, Tunisia has a strong Islamic faith and culture, which underpins the whole of society. In these challenging times for

1 CROATIA
2 BOSNIA & HERZEGOVINA
3 MONTENEGRO

the Muslim world, Tunisians have to balance their traditional values with modernity. Their greatest challenge is to keep strong ties with the Arab world while ensuring that the alliances that Tunis has developed in the Western world over many years are maintained.

Tunisia

History

Prehistory Up to 200,000 years ago, Stone Age people inhabited the area near Kelibia, on Cap Bon.

6000 BC The Sahara forms at the end of the Ice Age.

4500 BC Capsians arrive from the east. They settle near Gafsa, in the south.

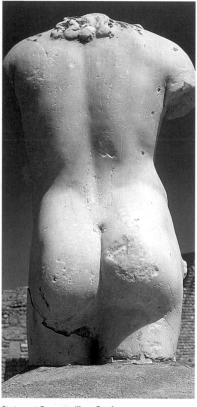

Statue at Roman villas, Carthage

1100–600 BC Carthage, Bizerte, Utica and Sousse are founded by the Phoenicians as staging posts on their trade route to Spain. Carthage becomes the centre of the Phoenicians' Tunisian empire, reaching its height in the 4th and 5th centuries BC.

600–300 BC Greeks and Carthaginians struggle for domination of the western Mediterranean.

264–241, 218–201, 149–146 BC The three Punic Wars, between Carthage and the new power of Rome, are fought. During the Second Punic War, Hannibal, the Carthaginian general, makes his famous march north with 300 elephants through France and over the Alps to attack Rome.

146 BC Carthage is ultimately defeated and then razed by Rome.

46 BC The Roman emperor Augustus starts to rebuild Carthage.

30 BC – AD 250 Under Roman rule, the country prospers and grows, extending southwards to Chott el-Jerid and westwards to Morocco.

200–312 Rise of Christianity in Africa, culminating in Christianity becoming the official religion of Roman Empire.

312–533 Disintegration and fall of the Roman Empire. In 439, the Vandals, a Germanic tribe, invade North Africa via Spain. They capture Carthage and put an end to Roman domination in Africa.

533–646 Byzantine rule is established by the emperor Justinian, from his capital Byzantium (modern Istanbul). Massive fortresses are built at Sbeïtla and Haïdra to control the rebellious native Berber population.

647–800 Under the banner of the new religion, Islam, Arab invaders enter the country from the east.

670 Okba ibn Nafaa al-Fihri founds Kairouan and makes Tunisia part of the new Umayyad Empire, which is ruled by caliphs from Damascus. Kairouan becomes the holiest city in the Maghreb.

800–909 Ibrahim ibn Aghlab declares himself governor and hereditary emir of Tunisia. He inaugurates the Golden Century of the Aghlabids, which is notable for its architectural achievements, including the walled médinas (town centres) and ribats (fortified monasteries) of Sousse and Monastir.

909–1229 A succession of Muslim dynasties – the Fatimids (Berber Shiites), Zirids, Moroccan Almohads and Almoravids – rule Tunisia. The infrastructure of the country collapses, leaving fragmented centres of population.

1230–1574 Tunis becomes the capital of the Hafsid dynasty. The country regains its trading role and re-establishes contact with Europe. Cultural life flourishes and many mosques are built in the Andalucian-influenced style that becomes Tunisia's architectural hallmark.

1534–74 Hispano-Turkish struggles predominate. Control of Tunis changes several times in quick succession and the Habsburg emperor Charles V puts a puppet Hafsid prince, Mulai-Hassan, on the throne, backed by Spanish troops.

1574–1881 Tunisia is made a regency of the Ottoman Empire, with hereditary beys (civil administrators) governing the cities of the coast and inland around Le Kef. The tribes in the south and the central plain, however, remain autonomous.

1861 Tunisia drafts the first constitution in the Arab world.

1881–1956 France occupies Tunisia, leaving the Bey as nominal ruler, but encouraging French immigration and the import of French goods. Primary education is limited to less than 10 per cent of the population, to ensure the continued role of Tunisians as labourers and servants.

1920 The Destour Party is formed and demands independence from the French. It is ignored.

1934 The Destour Party is powerless and in disarray. Habib Bourguiba founds the nationalist Neo-Destour Party. He is repeatedly arrested and exiled.

1956 France grants Tunisia full independence as a constitutional monarchy under Tunis Bey, the king.

1957 Habib ben Ali Bourguiba abolishes the monarchy.

1956–87 Bourguiba's presidency becomes a benevolent dictatorship, with widespread social reform. A moderate, non-aligned stance is adopted.

1959 Tunisia's constitution now dictates that the country's president must be a Muslim.

1987 Bourguiba is forced to retire. General Ben Ali assumes power in a bloodless palace coup and embarks on a policy of political liberalisation.

1999 Tunisia's first contested presidential election held.

2000	The death of Habib ben Ali Bourguiba. He is buried in Monastir after a muted funeral.
2001	Terrorist bomb in Jerba kills 20 tourists.
2004	President Ben Ali wins a fourth five-year term with 94 per cent of the vote.

Allegations of vote-rigging are rife.

2005	Parliament introduces an upper house dominated by the ruling party.
2006	Authorities launch campaign against the Islamic headscarves worn by some women.

The ruins of the Capitol Temple at Dougga

The land

Tunisia is the smallest of the five North African countries that are traditionally referred to as the Maghreb states. These countries – Morocco, Algeria, Tunisia, Libya and Mauritania – were given the name maghreb, meaning 'place of the sunset' in Arabic, because from the Arab heartland of Saudi Arabia they were viewed as the lands to the west, where the sun sets. Tunisia covers an area of 163,610sq km (63,170sq miles), a little more than England and Wales combined. Just 160km (99 miles) to the northeast, across the Mediterranean Sea, lies Sicily.

The landscape

Most of the country is low-lying, and its northern and eastern regions are bordered by coastal plains. While the northern coast is rocky, the eastern littoral has a gentle sandy coast known as the Sahel. It is here that the resorts are concentrated. The north, which is relatively mountainous, is dominated by the two easternmost ridges of the Atlas Mountains, the Northern Tell and the High Tell. The Mejerda river, which runs between them, is the only river in Tunisia to flow all year round. The Northern Tell is a continuation of the Algerian Tell Atlas, sandstone hills that rise no higher than 600m (2,000ft). The High Tell is a continuation of the Saharan Atlas, with rugged limestone and sandstone ridges. The highest peak, Jebel Chambi, rises to 1,544m (5,066ft) near the Algerian border. Tunisia's northern landscapes are surprisingly green and fertile, whereas south of the High Tell, the land becomes semi-desert

punctuated by occasional oases, such as those at Nefta and Tozeur.

Further south are the two great salt lakes (*chotts*), Chott el-Jerid and the Chott el-Gharsa, which respectively lie at 16m (52ft) and 21m (69ft) below sea level. South of the *chotts* the great Sahara desert begins. The edge of the dunes, known as the Grand Erg Oriental, is interrupted only by the flat-topped mountains, the Monts des Ksour, home of the Berber tribes.

Flora and fauna

Dates, citrus fruits, figs, bananas, tobacco and vegetables thrive in Tunisia's southern oases. The eastern coastal plain features an extensive swathe of olive groves, and smaller plantations of peach, apricot, almond and pomegranate trees. Subtropical plants such as bougainvillaea, oleander and hibiscus grow in profusion throughout the north and south. Lions, ostriches and antelopes were once among Tunisia's big animals, but now only the long-suffering dromedary remains. There are many species of smaller animals, however, and the birdlife around Cap Bon and the Gulf of Tunis is notable.

Climate

Northern Tunisia has a climate similar to the Mediterranean, with cool wet winters and hot dry summers. Rainfall is especially high over the northern mountains, allowing oak trees to flourish in the more remote hills and crops to be grown in the lowlands without the need for irrigation.

South of the Tell, the only vegetation on the plains is clumps of esparto grass, which is collected and exported for paper manufacture, and the only population centres are in the oases where underground water supplies allow cultivation, notably the famous date palms of Nefta, Tozeur and Gafsa. The southern interior experiences extremes of temperature by day and night, high winds and very little rainfall. At Tozeur, in July for example, the daytime temperature may reach 40°C (104°F) and drop to below zero at night.

The island of Jerba enjoys year-round sunshine, making it a popular winter holiday destination, while in summer, sea breezes allay the extreme heat. Hardier visitors claim that the sea off Jerba is swimmable even in December.

The land

The Northern Tell is a mountainous region, with green and fertile valleys

Culture

Tunisia is the most European of the Arab nations. The French colonial influence still lingers, but the country's strongest links are definitely with the Islamic world. However, it is one of the most liberal of Arab countries.

Origins

After 30,000 BC, the sea level in the Mediterranean rose, separating North Africa from Europe, and causing indigenous cultures to develop independently in Tunisia. Of these cultures, the most advanced was the Capsian, which is named after the oasis of Gafsa, ancient Capsa, where archaeologists discovered finely crafted stone tools, along with knives and needles made from bone, and necklaces made from ostrich eggs. The finds were dated to 7000–4500 BC. Over thousands of years, the indigenous Capsians interbred and integrated with Berbers, Phoenicians, Romans, Byzantines and Arabs. The Arab culture that was imposed on Tunisia in the 7th century has predominated ever since, so that modern Tunisians regard themselves as North African Arabs. Small numbers of Berbers survive in isolated pockets in the south. The Muslim Hafsid dynasty, which ruled Tunisia for almost 300 years from 1230 to 1500, established

Tunis as the country's capital. This was also the period when Tunisia's contemporary Arabic identity developed most strongly.

Character

The modern Tunisian character has been heavily influenced by 75 years of French colonial rule, from 1881 to 1956. During that period, the healthcare reforms introduced by the French were so effective that the country's population grew from 1 million to 4 million. Today, Tunisia is a young country where over half the inhabitants are under 20.

The French set up new schools and French-style commercial enterprises with the result that, in the cities especially, a veneer of sophistication is apparent, along with a high tolerance of foreigners. One of the things that will strike visitors to Tunisia when they encounter it is the Arab sense of hospitality, which is remarkably open and generous.

Livelihood

Tunisia's major industry is tourism. However, despite its popular image as a hot, sun-baked country, over 60 per cent of the land is suitable for agriculture. Cereals are grown in the fertile northern valleys, while on Cap Bon, in the far northeast, the soil is especially suitable for cultivating citrus fruits. Olive trees flourish in the Sahel, along the eastern coast. The country's interior is filled with pastureland and the oases of the south are famous for their dates. Farming therefore occupies the bulk of the country's non-urban population, with fishing and tourism being the main sources of income along the coast.

Modern society

In the past the bedrock of Tunisian society was the extended family, which could be relied on to provide financial support and practical aid in times of need. Personal identity was strongly linked to family, with the extended family growing to encompass people of the same lineage or tribe and from the same village. These wider groupings were given cohesion by a common sense of honour and pride in their members' achievements and reputations, and a corresponding sense of shame if honour was besmirched.

However, with the increasing movement of Tunisians away from the villages and their rural lives, and into towns and cities, this complex web of traditional social cohesion is under great strain, and frequently breaks down altogether. Earnings, which are roughly equal in rural society, diverge widely in towns and cities, and a sense of obligation to the other clan members is seen as less important. Customs and ceremonies also lose their relevance in an urban setting. It is only in the villages that lively traditional weddings, with musicians and singers, still take place. Another traditional celebration that shows signs of decline is the *ziara*, an annual outing to the tomb of a local *marabout* (holy man), which used to bring the whole community together once a year. It was also at these gatherings that marriages would be arranged and family ties reasserted.

Against the background of these changes, which have been brought about primarily by economic need, is another social development, that of the changing role and needs of women. With access to birth control and higher education, women are questioning their traditional place in modern Tunisian society.

A cheerful welcome for tourists at their refreshments stop near Tamerza

Festivals

A Muslim country, Tunisia celebrates Islamic feast days. Friday is the holy day of the week, although Sunday is the official holiday, when souks, offices and banks are closed. The two major annual festivals, when everything shuts down for three days, are the Eid el-Kebir, commemorating Abraham's willingness to sacrifice his son Isaac, and the Eid es-Saghir, which marks the end of Ramadan, the month of fasting. Family visits and eating are the main activities during these festivities. Each year the date of these festivals changes as they are fixed to the lunar calendar.

Tunisia also has a rich tradition of local festivals, most of which take place in July and August. Although most festivals have their roots in a local tradition or event, many festivals are gradually changing to accommodate the tourist market. Local tourist offices should be able to supply you with a programme of events.

April Nabeul Festival of Oranges, coinciding with the orange-blossom season, with a programme of cultural events aimed at tourists rather than native Tunisians.

May/June El-Haouaria Falconry Festival, a series of competitions in which falcons are released to catch partridge and quail. The falcons are caught in March or April, on their migration route through Cap Bon, then trained by villagers for the festival before being released.

June Testour Festival of Malouf Music,

held in the large café below the Great Mosque. Andalucian-based folk music.

July/August Sousse Festival of Theatre and Music, a programme of cultural events for tourists, including folk music and dancing.

July/August Dougga Festival of Classical Theatre, featuring classic French plays.

July/August Kerkennah Folklore Festival, an event for tourists.

July/August Hammamet International Cultural Festival, with musical and dramatic performances in French and Arabic. These are held in the mock-Greek theatre in the grounds of George Sebastian's villa.

July/August Carthage International Cultural Festival, the largest cultural festival in Tunisia. Staged in the restored Roman theatre at Carthage, and including dance, cinema, theatre and music. Most events are in French and are advertised in the press and on billboards. Tickets can be bought at the Roman theatre.

July/August Jerba Folklore Festival, biennial (odd years).

July/August Tabarka International Cultural Festival, which is attended by hundreds of students. There are also evening events, which include debates, reviews, art and music.

July/August Gabès Festival of Sidi Boulbaba, named after the saint who was the Prophet Muhammad's barber, with cultural and folklore events.

August Monastir Theatre and Poetry Festival, a cultural event with performances mainly in French.

November Kebili, a date-harvest festival.

November Carthage International Film Festival, with Arab and African films. A biennial event, this festival takes over Tunis' cinemas every other November (odd years). The shows are listed in the French daily newspapers.

December/January Tozeur Folklore Festival, with camel races and various Bedouin spectacles.

December/January Douz National Sahara Festival, featuring such oddities as camel fights, sand hockey and greyhound racing. Music, poetry and singing are also included.

Colourful musicians and dancers perform at Douz's Festival of the Sahara

Politics

Tunisia has been a republic since 1956, when it gained independence from French colonial rule and when its first president, Habib Bourguiba, effectively created modern Tunisia. Ben Ali, the current president, has been in office since 1987, when he seized power from Bourguiba.

The National Assembly is elected every five years by direct universal suffrage of all citizens over the age of 20. The president is head of state and commander-in-chief of the army. The president's party, the Constitutional Democratic Rally (CRD), is the dominant one, other parties playing a largely peripheral role. The country is divided into 23 governorates (*wilayas*), each with a governor who reports directly to the president.

Political reforms

Although Habib Bourguiba initiated many reforms, including outlawing polygamy, giving women equal rights and moderating of the influence of Islam on Tunisian society, this has with time been eroded because of world events. The effect of the terrorist attacks on the United States on 11 September 2001 and the rise of Islamic fundamentalism have meant that President Ben Ali has deemed it necessary to impose a quasi-police

state to maintain peace. Stability and a buoyant economy (compared to that of other North African countries) are Ben Ali's major achievement. According to government statistics, 60 per cent of Tunisians are middle class. But all this has been achieved at the cost of press freedom and allegedly of democracy, too.

The bad human rights record that Tunisia suffered under President Bourguiba continues under President Ben Ali. According to the president, such strictures are necessary in order to control extremism in the Arab world.

President Ben Ali was due to retire in 2004, but in 2002 he won popular support for changes to the constitution that now permit him to run for two further terms in office. In contested elections, he has repeatedly won nearly all votes. In recent elections, accusations of vote-rigging have been rife, and censorship of the foreign press has been widespread. Two days before the 2004 presidential elections, the

Democratic Progressive Party pulled out of the contest, alleging illegalities in counting procedures.

Foreign relations

Since it won independence, Tunisia has adopted a moderate, non-aligned stance. Habib Bourguiba initiated this policy and Ben Ali has continued it.

Ben Ali has improved relations between Tunisia and its neighbour, Libya, which was on the brink of declaring war on Tunisia in 1985. There is now freedom of movement between these countries, and Tunisians may work in Libya, and Libyans in Tunisia. As a result of this, large numbers of Tunisians work in Libya's oil industry and other areas. Relations with Algeria, however, are still strained.

Despite the Iraq War of 2003, relations between Tunisia and the United States have not suffered significantly. In fact, the United States' support for Israel is a greater barrier to diplomatic harmony between the two countries. Although the Tunisian government did not support Saddam Hussein, the former Iraqi president, the country is divided on the invasion of Iraq that deposed him, even though it did not officially oppose the United States too strongly. Demonstrations against the war in Iraq were quickly quashed, and the police charged an antiwar demonstration in Sfax.

Relations between Tunisia and the brotherhood of Arab countries is generally good and the country is seen as having a unifying and peacekeeping influence in the region, although some Arab leaders consider Tunisian policies to be too liberal and too pro-Western. In 2005, Tunisia hosted a UN conference on the Global Information Society, during which there were allegations, denied by the authorities, that police harassed journalists and other delegates. In 2006, Tunisia moved to close its embassy in Qatar in protest at alleged bias by the Qatar-based TV channel Al-Jazeera.

Tunisia is part of the Arab Maghreb Union, whose other members are Algeria, Morocco, Libya and Mauritania. This body encourages trade between its member countries. Relations between Tunisia and the European Union, particularly with France, are also good. Most of Tunisia's exports are to the EU and most tourists are from within the EU.

The omnipresent posters of President Ben Ali, Tunisia's leader since 1987

Islam in Tunisia

Islamic graves and headstones are very simple

Islam, which means 'submission to God' in Arabic, is one of the world's three great monotheistic religions, along with Judaism and Christianity. Islam acknowledges the prophets of both Judaism and Christianity, including Jesus, although it does not recognise him as the Son of God.

The Islamic faith was established in the early 7th century, when Muhammad, a merchant from Mecca, heard Allah (God) speaking to him. These divine messages were transcribed to form the Koran (meaning 'Recitation'), which sets out the rules of behaviour and the social order for all Muslims. (The 30-day fast of Ramadan, when Muslims must not eat, drink or smoke from dawn to dusk, does not usually present a problem for visitors to Tunisia, and restaurants do remain open in all the resorts.)

Tunisian Muslims belong almost exclusively to the moderate, orthodox Sunni branch of Islam, the only exceptions being the Kharijite sect on Jerba and the Sufi (mystic) sect in Nefta. After a drop in mosque attendances in the 1950s and 1960s, Islam in Tunisia has recently seen a revival, with full mosques, often with young congregations, and many new mosques being built. The reason for this revival is thought to be a reaction against the speedy process of Westernisation that Tunisia underwent under President Bourguiba, which brought materialism and corruption in its wake. A return to spiritual Islamic values has given the young a focus for their frustrations and a sense of identity.

Islamic fundamentalism

Like every moderate Arab state, Tunisia has feared the spread of the Iranian-style Islamic revolution, and Islamic fundamentalists were banned as early as 1979. Shortly before the 1981 elections the Mouvement de la Tendence Islamique (MTI) was formed, only to be banned almost immediately, and its leaders imprisoned. Under General Ben Ali the policy was at first to relax political censorship, and the MTI, now called En-Nahda (the Renaissance) was tolerated, and there was even talk of legalising it as a party. However, when in 1990 the Islamic fundamentalists won a massive victory in the Algerian municipal elections, fear set in again, with ensuing repression, the banning of En-Nahda, widespread arrests and even executions. The new wave of repressions has led to protests from international human-rights groups, and France in particular has voiced disapproval of the censorship of certain French newspapers and the expulsion of French journalists. President Ben Ali's reaction was to denounce foreign journalists and human-rights groups for interfering in Tunisia's internal affairs, while at the same time ensuring that Tunisia's image as a liberal holiday playground was unsullied.

A traditional-style mosque in Jerba

Impressions

The tourist areas of Tunisia will not prove to be much of a culture shock for most Europeans. They cater well for holidaymakers. Being aware of local customs and mores will enhance your stay.

Body language and dress

In a Muslim country like Tunisia it is important to realise that different codes of dress and behaviour apply. A little bit of carelessness can cause considerable offence. A modern country, Tunisia is not as conservative as other Arab countries. However, you can still induce the wrath of a local inhabitant if you show too much exposed flesh. This applies both to male and female visitors. Nudity of any sort is not advised, even in *hammams* (steam baths), where most Tunisians stay partially attired and keep their private areas covered. In resort areas, etiquette is considerably more relaxed. Here some foreign visitors can even bathe topless without too much hassle, but this shouldn't be done on public beaches. Observing etiquette shows respect for local sensibilities and beliefs and ensures that your interaction with local people is cordial and pleasant. In towns and cities, beachwear is not really considered acceptable. Long-sleeved, free-flowing cotton clothing is best for both sexes. In rural areas, local people are even more conservative, and you need to be aware of this.

It is imperative to dress appropriately when you are going near a mosque. Do not attempt to enter a mosque in shorts or skimpy clothing as to a Tunisian this shows the utmost disrespect.

Public embracing or kissing between adults of the opposite sex is generally considered taboo, but is probably tolerated in most areas now. Again if you don't do it, you won't offend. Strangely to Westerners, this show of affection is, however, perfectly acceptable between men greeting each other. Blowing your nose in public is also considered offensive.

If you want to take a photograph of someone, it is polite to ask them first, and not to persist if they decline.

Mosques

In Tunisia, as in most other Arab countries, only Muslims may enter the prayer hall of a mosque. Non-Muslims can, however, enter the courtyards of three mosques (a fee is payable). These are the Zitouna Mosque in Tunis, the Great Mosque in Kairouan and the Great Mosque in Sousse.

Even on shopping trips to buy some pottery, the woman's place is a few steps behind

Women travellers

For women, travelling in Tunisia is certainly much more comfortable than it once was. It is still better for a woman to travel with a man or another female companion. If you are a woman travelling alone, it is best to dress conservatively to avoid any situations that may cause problems, and to be on the alert for any signs of malign intent in over-attentive males. Crimes against women are rare in Tunisia (as in all Muslim countries), but they may be subjected to unpleasant looks and verbal harassment. There is a misconception among some Tunisian men that a Western woman travelling alone is of easy virtue and available.

Women travelling alone have the advantage that they can join in the local social gatherings of Tunisian women in the *hammams*. This is a place where all cultural barriers are forsaken and where some great friendships between people of different nationalities are struck.

Culture shock

Tunisia is not really a place that should cause too much of a culture shock to travellers who have been to an Arab country before. It is one of the easiest Arabic countries to travel in and the

local people are now well used to foreigners. You may attract a lot of attention in the remote areas, but will not get a second glance if you dress acceptably in the resort towns or cities. One thing that tourists, especially vegetarians, may find offensive, are the meat markets, so if you are squeamish avoid these areas in the médina. You may find the head of a cow suddenly staring back at you.

Smoking is a way of life among Tunisian males, and any suggestion that it be curbed in public places will not go down well. At least the climate permits outdoor seating for most of the year.

MUSEUMS AND SITES

Monday is the commonest closing day, with usual opening hours Tuesday to Sunday 9am–noon, 2–5.30pm winter, 3–6.30pm summer. There is almost always an additional fee for using a camera.

The country's most famous and impressive museum is the Bardo, the National Archaeological Museum in Tunis (*see pp28–9*). After this, the best museums are housed in restored town houses like the 17th-century Dar Jellouli in Sfax (*see pp76–7*) and the 18th-century Dar Ben Abdallah in Tunis (*see pp30–31*).

The regions

Tunisia has such geographic diversity that you may think you are entering another country when you go from region to region. The rolling hills of the North are like parts of Spain or Italy, and miles of sandy beaches line the coast. In the South, the magical barren Sahara desert dominates the Southern interior with the only respite being in desert oasis towns that seem trapped in another era.

Tunis and the north

Tunis, the country's capital, is located in a sheltered inlet on the north coast, where the coastline holds many surprises for the first-time visitor. Rugged and rocky for the most part, it also has some beautiful deserted sandy coves, which can be visited either from the resort of Tabarka, near the Algerian border, or from the attractive old city of Bizerte.

Tunis itself is one of the most sophisticated Arab capitals, the French colonial influence still apparent in its wide boulevards and shopping malls. Tourists visit Tunis mainly for its old

The rocky shoreline at the tip of Cap Bon, near El-Haouaria

The fertility of an oasis

médina, the original 13th-century walled city that holds the *souks* (oriental bazaars) in narrow alleyways round the central Zitouna Mosque. The city's other great attraction is the Bardo, the national museum, housed in a 19th-century beylical palace in one of the city's outer suburbs. It is world-famous for its Roman mosaics.

Further out, scattered among the wealthy residential suburbs, lies the scant remains of Carthage, one of ancient history's most evocative names, while just next door is Sidi Bou Said, often cited as the prettiest village in Tunisia. Inland, in the fertile rolling hills of the Mejerda river valley, lie intriguing Roman remains, most notably the underground villas of Bulla Regia.

Cap Bon and the coastal plain

Cap Bon is the peninsula that juts out into the Mediterranean in Tunisia's northeastern corner. Covered in citrus plantations and vineyards, it is somewhat similar to southern Italy. The coastal plain, starting at Nabeul and Hammamet and running south to Gabès, is known as the Sahel (Arabic for 'coast') or the Olive Coast. The Sahel has Tunisia's finest beaches and resorts, as well as the four ancient walled cities of Sousse, Mahdia, Sfax and Kairouan, which contain fascinating examples of Islamic architecture. Inland the scenery is flat and monotonous, with countless olive groves and prickly pears. The contrast between the hubbub of the major beach resorts and the tranquil rural scenes not far inland is striking.

Tamerza Gorge in the south

of relaxation. Should you wish to leave the beach, you are well placed for inland excursions to the fascinating Berber village strongholds of Chenini and Guermessa, or to the weird moonscapes of the Matmata region, with its troglodytic dwellings. For the intrepid, camel treks and safaris by four-wheel-drive vehicle can be organised into the desert to experience the Grand Erg Oriental, the edge of the African Sahara.

The interior

Further inland the landscape becomes increasingly rugged and mountainous. These highlands of the interior, known as the Tell (Arabic for 'hill'), are where many of Tunisia's most spectacular Roman ruins are to be found – Dougga, Sbeïtla, Makthar, Medeina and Haïdra – often in rugged and beautiful settings. The key city of the Tell is Le Kef, an intriguing place with a totally different character from that of the coastal cities. The southern part of the interior also has some magnificent natural phenomena, including the oases of Tamerza, Nefta and Tozeur, the Selja Gorge, and the salt lake of Chott el-Jerid, an eerie, alien landscape traversed by a causeway.

Jerba and the south

Closer in feel to the Sahara than to the Mediterranean, the southern part of the country features the resorts of the Île de Jerba (Island of Jerba), where sun-lovers and 'lotos-eaters' come in search

Getting around
Bus

This is the cheapest form of travel but timetables and networks are often so complicated it's not worth the bother.

Car hire

If you want to tour Tunisia's sites and your time is limited, car hire is by far the best option. It is expensive by European standards, so it is worth shopping around in your own country, and on the Internet, to find the best deal. However, be wary of the attractive

---

THOMAS COOK'S TUNISIA

Thomas Cook first began organising tours to Tunisia in 1895, as part of a 33-day tour from Paris and Marseille that covered Algeria and Tunisia together. By 1902 its business had grown to the point where an office was opened in Tunis, from which it offered excursions to Carthage, Kairouan and the baths of Hammam-Meskoutine. In 1904 a four-week tour to Algeria and Tunisia from London cost 60 guineas, first class, all inclusive.

The regions

lower rates offered by small local firms, as the standard of their cars and the quality of their service in the event of breakdown can often be less than satisfactory.

Louage

Louages are shared taxis, which run on set routes between towns throughout the country. They set off either when they have their quota of five passengers or when the driver thinks that no one else will arrive. The most difficult thing about using *louages* is finding their departure point, especially in large towns, where they vary according to destination. Once that hurdle is overcome (just asking around is the best way), the rest is relatively easy. Prices are fixed and low, although you may have to battle your way through to get in. *Louages* hurtle around at great speed, reaching their destination considerably faster than you are likely to in your hired car.

Taxi

Yellow taxis are the best way of travelling around towns and cities. They are metered, although it is imperative to check that the driver has actually turned the meter on, thus obviating tension or disputes later. At peak times (noon–3pm and 5–7pm), taxis are scarce, especially in Tunis. This is partly because demand is highest then and partly because that is when the taxi drivers take their meal breaks.

Train

Tunisian railways are efficient, with air-conditioned comfort in first class, and surprisingly good sandwiches. The stations are well kept and prices are cheap. The main disadvantage is that there are only four main routes, so many smaller places are not linked by the railway network. From Tunis these four routes are: north to Bizerte (1 hour 50 minutes); west to the Algerian border at Ghardimao via Béja and Jendouba (about 6 hours); southwest into the Tell through El-Fahs and Dahmani, with an offshoot to Le Kef (about 6 hours); and south to Gabès, via Hammamet, Sousse, El-Jem and Sfax, with offshoots to Gafsa, Monastir and Mahdia (the journey to Gabès takes about 9 hours, and involves changing twice). Tunis also has its own underground 'metro' system.

Outside the cities, the road quality is good and they are nearly empty of traffic

Tunis

Modern Tunis makes light of its 3,000-year-old history and presents a sophisticated, liberal capital despite its obvious Arab heritage and allegiances. It was the 7th-century Arab conquest that brought about the transformation of Tunis from a minor lakeside town to a wealthy trading city.

Egyptian workers were used to dig a 10km- (6-mile-) long canal from Tunis to the sea at what is now called La Goulette, and the city subsequently developed into the principal seaport between Europe and Africa. The most prosperous period of all was under the Hafsid dynasty (1230–1574), when the population rose to 100,000 and the Jemaa ez Zitouna (Zitouna Mosque), together with its dependent *madrasas* (theological colleges), grew to be one of the great North African universities.

Destruction and decline followed in the 16th century, when in the course of the Habsburg–Ottoman war, Tunis was seized and the Zitouna Mosque used as

Statue of Ibn Khan in Tunis

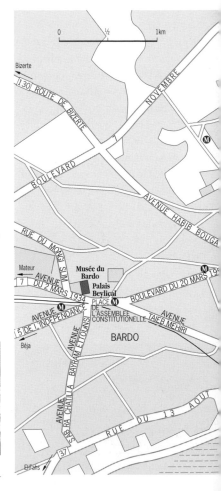

stables by the Habsburgs. Its library and sacred tombs were vandalised and destroyed. Over the ensuing centuries, the old walled médina of Tunis was increasingly neglected in favour of the colonial New Town, built on land reclaimed from the lake, thereby creating the divide that still exists today. The population of Tunis is now about 2 million, a fifth of the whole country's, and, as the seat of government and centre of all industries except mining, it is the undisputed chief city.

For most tourists who visit from their beach resorts, Tunis means little more than shopping in the *souks* and a quick trip out to the Bardo and/or Sidi Bou Said. Travellers with a little more time, however, can uncover much more, particularly in the old médina.

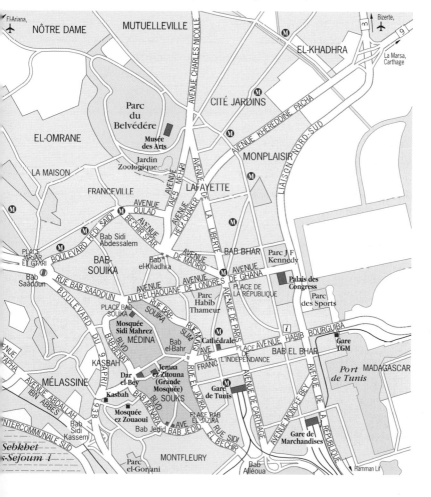

The Bardo

The Bardo was one of the new palaces built in the 18th century by the Husseinite rulers, who favoured outlying locations on hilltops rather than the old médina. The médina was used only for their final resting place, the Tourbet el-Bey, which is now the recommended M'rabet café and restaurant. As Tunisia's national museum, the Musée du Bardo is the repository of the country's archaeological treasures. But it is visited primarily for its mosaics, one of the most impressive collections in the world, taken from various Roman sites around the country.

Downstairs

The downstairs rooms display a large collection of sarcophagi, stelae and statues from the Carthaginian and Roman periods. In Room A, look out for the splendid 1st-century AD terracotta statue of Baal Hammon, chief god of Carthage, sitting on a throne and wearing an unusual feathered headdress. Note the magnificent sarcophagi of the Muses opposite the door of Room V. In Room VIII you will find a pair of gigantic arms that belonged to a cult statue of Jupiter found at Thuburbo Majus. The feet of this statue are to be found upstairs among the artefacts from Sousse. Another exceptional exhibit in this area is the 3rd-century AD mosaic of Perseus and Andromeda with the sea monster, which is in Room VI. It was taken from an underground villa at Bulla Regia.

Mosaic detail

A cupola mosaic in the Bardo

Upstairs

The main staircase leads up to the Arab Museum, a curious museum within a museum, with exhibits of calligraphy and swords. The building itself is in fact the main attraction, with a tiled courtyard, glass roof to the sky, superbly carved woodwork and elaborate plasterwork. The stairs continue up to the main mosaic exhibits, laid out on the floors and walls of the colossal palace banqueting rooms, which still retain some of their pink chandeliers. Many of the mosaics show commonly portrayed Roman themes, such as the sea, the gods and hunting scenes. The mosaics that stand out by virtue

of their different subject matter are in the Hadrumete Room and show 'lord-of-the-manor' type houses set in their estates, giving a rare insight into the domestic architecture of the 4th century AD. In one scene, the master and mistress are sitting outside the manor, and the whole image is strikingly modern.

Right at the back, on the wall of Room XV, is the 3rd-century AD mosaic of the poet Virgil with Clio, Muse of History. Small but in excellent condition, with strong sharp colours, it is generally regarded as Tunisia's most famous mosaic. It was found in a villa in Sousse.

Further stairs lead up to the top-floor gallery, which has rather less dramatic displays of pottery, glass and bronze, and which most people give a miss, especially if their energy or interest is flagging.

6km (3½ miles) from central Tunis on the Bizerte road, near the Gare du 20 Mars on Boulevard du 20 Mars 1956. Open: Tuesday to Sunday 9.30am–4.30pm in winter; 9am–5pm in summer. Admission charge – extra charge for photography; the use of camera flash and tripods is forbidden. There are many steps, even between sections on the same floor, and the museum is therefore quite unsuitable for small children, pushchairs, the elderly and people with disabilities.

The médina

The original centre of Tunis is the walled city known as the médina, which dates back to the 9th century. The main building surviving from this period is the Zitouna Mosque. The médina remained the heart of the city's commercial life until the 18th and 19th centuries, when new European factories were built on the outskirts and began to eat away at the traditional markets.

In 1861, the *bey* (ruler) ordered the medieval walls to be taken down, and by the early 20th century the old médina had become an overcrowded, run-down slum housing some 300,000 Tunisians. Meanwhile, the 150,000 or so Europeans lived out in the spacious New Town, which was served by new hospitals, banks and schools. In 1956, when the French and Italians left after independence, many of the merchant traders moved out of the old médina and into the newly vacated villas and flats, leaving much of the médina empty for rural immigrants.

Today the médina remains an anachronism, a collection of medieval alleyways in the heart of modern Tunis. It is the city's main tourist attraction for precisely that reason. Tunis' major Islamic monuments all lie within the médina. Non-Muslims can visit only three of them: the Zitouna Mosque, the Museum Dar Ben Abdallah and the Dar Othman. The functioning mosques, *madrasas* and *zaouias*

(Islamic religious schools) remain firmly closed to tourists. The médina is pedestrianised, although a few persistent merchants' vehicles squeeze along its narrow alleys. A ring road, which follows the line of the now-vanished defensive walls, runs around the médina.

Dar Ben Abdallah (Museum of Arts and Traditions)
A visit to the 18th-century palace museum will probably be one of the highlights of your visit to Tunis, both for the beauty of the building itself, and for the peace it offers from the hurly-burly of the street life just outside (*see map, p35*). In the summer months you will be astonished by the coolness of the rooms, achieved solely through the courtyard ventilation design, which maximises air movement. The dark entrance corridor, lined with benches, is where callers would wait their turn to be summoned for an audience with the noble master of the household. The

four rooms off the courtyard contain beautiful exhibits of models dressed in traditional costumes, including a men's gathering, bridal preparations, babywear and sequinned circumcision suits. Notice especially the lovely painted wooden ceilings and the tilework, plus the many wells surrounded by exquisite coloured marblework.

Two streets, the Rue du Riche and Rue des Andalous, run between the Dar Ben Abdallah and the Zitouna Mosque. They feature the domestic architecture of the médina at its most elegant, with carved stone pillars, fine studded doors, vaulted passageways and arched gateways, leaving you to guess at the splendour of the 17th-century palaces and gardens within.

Rue Sidi Kassem. Open: Mon–Sat 9.30am–4.30pm. Admission charge.

Souks in the médina of Tunis

The médina

The minaret of Tunis' Zitouna Mosque as seen from the roof terrace in the *souk*

Dar Othman

Dating from the 17th century, the Dar Othman is a palace in a different style from that of the Dar Ben Abdallah; it is smaller and also has a pretty garden courtyard. Visitors can enter the courtyards (*see map, p35*).
Rue El-Mekhtar.

MOSQUES AND *MADRASAS*

Apart from the Zitouna, none of the other mosques mentioned here can be visited by non-Muslims, and the closest you can get is a view inside the Mosquée Sidi Youssef (Mosque of Sidi Youssef) from the rooftop terrace of the Musée des Turcs, an antique shop in the Souk el-Trouk. Built in 1616, its elegant octagonal minaret is the oldest Turkish-style minaret in the city, and is completely separate from the prayer hall. In Rue des Librairies, a short walk south from the mosque end of Rue Jemaa ez Zitouna, is a cluster of three 18th-century *madrasas* – En-Nakhla, Bachiya and Slimanyia – but the most you can do is catch a glimpse of the courtyards if someone happens to be opening the gate. The other mosque to look out for is the Mosquée de la Kasbah (Kasbah Mosque). Built in the mid-13th century by the Hafsids, its minaret is the highest in the city.

Jemaa Ez Zotouna (Zitouna Mosque)

This is the spiritual heart of the city and the only mosque in Tunis that non-Muslims can visit. Even here, however, you are not allowed into the prayer hall and can only view the exterior from the courtyard. The present mosque was originally built in the 9th century. The name Zitouna (meaning 'olive tree') refers to the tree on the site, under which the original founder used to stand and preach. The oldest stones, taken from the city of Carthage after the Romans rebuilt it, are in the high outer wall. The prayer hall and the colonnaded courtyard both date from the 9th century, while the present tall, heavy minaret was built as late as 1894.

In its heyday, under the Hafsid dynasty in the 13th to 15th centuries, *madrasas* were built on to the mosque, and the reputation of the Zitouna as a university equalled even that of Egypt's élite Al-Azhar at that time. The prayer hall was also used as a lecture hall and up to 10,000 students used to attend lectures here in the 1950s.

Teaching only stopped at the Zitouna in 1960, when the study of the Koran and of Islamic jurisprudence was transferred to the new National University of Tunis. Despite the fact that entry to the prayer hall is prohibited for non-Muslims, from the outside the Zitouna still manages to convey a special atmosphere of peace and tranquillity, far removed from the chaotic mêlée of *souks* just outside its walls.
Rue Jemaa ez Zitouna. Open: Sat–Thur, 8am–noon. Admission charge. Photography permitted from the balustrade.

Walk: Old and new Tunis

This is an easy walk from the New Town of Tunis, into the medieval world of the médina. It should preferably be done in the morning, when the mosque is open and the souks are at their liveliest. Allow one hour for walking, plus additional time for browsing in the souks.

Start in Place de l'Indépendance.

1 Cathédrale de St Vincent de Paul

The French built this amazing neo-Gothic cathedral in 1882. There is a large bust of God on the roof. Directly opposite stands the French Embassy, built in colonial times as the office of the resident French governor.
Follow the tree-lined Avenue de France westwards, looking along the elegant arcades that house Tunis' most sophisticated shops.

2 Place de la Victoire

Avenue de France ends in the small Place de la Victoire, recognisable by the Bab el-Bahr, an arched gateway that was once the sea gate of the old city wall but now stands incongruously in the centre of the square. On the north is the handsome green and white stucco façade of the British Embassy, with the British Council library on the ground floor.
From Bab el-Bahr follow Rue Jemaa ez Zitouna, the main street of the médina.

3 Rue Jemaa ez Zitouna

Here you will find yourself sucked into the seething mass that is medieval Tunis. You will be hailed from all sides by shopkeepers vying with each other to lure you into their shops, and be bewildered by the variety of noises, colours and smells that suddenly bombard your senses. For most, it is something of a relief to emerge into daylight in front of the high walls of the Jemaa ez Zitouna (Grande Mosquée).

4 Jemaa ez Zitouna

The entrance to the mosque is up the steps to your left. The tranquillity of its courtyard offers a welcome respite from the médina. The Zitouna Mosque is surrounded on all sides by *souks*, and so long as you remember this it is virtually impossible to get lost.
Descend the mosque steps, turn left and go back past Rue Jemaa ez Zitouna. Turn left again around the corner of the mosque wall into Souk el-Attarine.

5 Souk el-Attarine

This is the 13th-century Perfumiers'
Market, with stalls laden with tiny
bottles of exquisite scent.
*At the next junction turn left into the
Souk des Étoffes.*

6 Souk des Étoffes

Make a stop here to shop in the Cloth
Market, with its red and green painted
columns, or if you want a tea or coffee,
continue straight on uphill into the
Souk el-Trouk (Market of the Turks),

where you will find the authentically
Tunisian M'rabet Café on your right.
This is a good place to relax, sitting
either inside on the raised benches
covered in rush matting, or out in the
little garden.
*Returning to the Souk des Étoffes,
continue your circuit of the mosque
through the souks, until you have
returned to the front entrance. Retrace
your steps down Rue Jemaa ez Zitouna
until you find yourself back at your
starting point.*

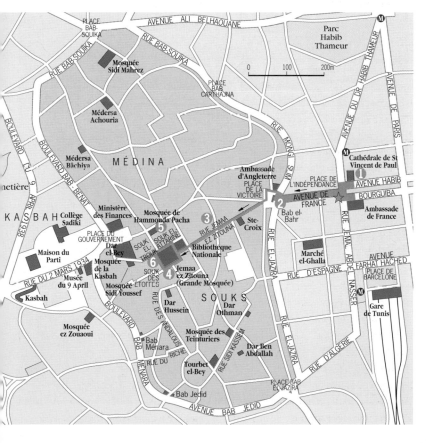

Souks

Souks, the traditional trading areas common to all Arabic countries, are located in the médina, the old centre of major towns. Tunis, Sousse, Kairouan, Hammamet and Houmt-Souk each have extensive and authentic *souks*. The *souk* in Tunis is the largest in Tunisia and is still central to life in the city, despite the fact this is also a modern Arabic city.

Souks usually consist of a maze of covered alleyways and narrow lanes

A classic-patterned rug

Perfume seller

and the Souk des Étoffes, with cascading cloth and materials. Also nearby is the Souk el-Blaghia (Slipper-Makers' Market) and the Souk el-Trouk (Market of the Turks, since the tailors who made the caftan-style robes here were Turkish).

The Souk des Orfèvres (Goldworkers' Market) is still the centre for jewellery, and beautifully painted booths are to be found there. In the Souk Sekkajine you will find carpet shops such as the famous Palais d'Orient, also known as the Maison d'Orient, with its panoramic roof terrace. This *souk* also boasts some beautiful embroidery stalls. Kilim-style (flatwoven) carpets are found in Souk el-Leffa. For the finest leatherwork, go to Souk el-Dzira. The more polluting trades, such as tanning, dyeing and metalworking, are to be found in outlying *souks*, which are further away from the Zitouna Mosque.

These days, especially along the main streets of the *souk*, the tradition of segregating various trades has largely broken down as a result of many larger shops offering tourists a range of souvenirs all under one roof. Prices (which are never fixed anywhere in the *souk*) will be highest in these shops, so unless you are very pushed for time, make the effort to find the more authentic specialist shops just off the main road.

that seem chaotic and confusing. They are in fact very ordered, with shops grouped according to trade in areas assigned to each trade. Hence copperware is found in one part of the *souk*, while perfumes are elsewhere. The most refined or cleanest trades are usually located closest to the mosque. This is why the Zitouna Mosque in Tunis is surrounded by the Souk el-Attarine (Perfumiers' Market, scent-making being the most refined trade of all)

TUNIS ENVIRONS
Carthage

Carthage, one of the most famous and romantic names from antiquity, is today a peaceful up-market commuter suburb of Tunis. The glory that was Carthage has long gone and only scattered ruins mark what was once the powerhouse of the Phoenicians' Tunisian empire and then of Rome's North African empire.

According to legend, Carthage was founded in 814 BC by Phoenicians from Tyre led by Queen Dido. By the 4th century BC Carthage had grown to become the great trading centre of the Phoenician maritime empire and was the most important city in the Mediterranean, if not in the Classical world. Its pre-eminence was not to last long, however, and conflict with Rome led to the Punic Wars of 264–241 BC, 218–201 BC and 149–146 BC. The Roman senator Cato the Elder famously declared that '*Delenda est Carthago*' ('We must destroy Carthage'), an aim that Rome finally accomplished in 146 BC. Carthage was sacked, its buildings razed to the ground, its soil ploughed and salt poured on it to render it useless for growing crops.

One hundred years later the Roman emperor Augustus decided to build a new city on the site – Colonia Julia Carthago. In due course this became the capital of Roman Africa and a great centre of learning and commerce. It is the ruins of this Roman city that we can still see today. Roman Carthage itself fell into ruin after the Arab conquest in AD 692, and its stones were used to build the médina in Tunis.

The site

At least one entire day is needed to see the whole of Carthage. However, few people have the time or the stamina for the lengthy hiking involved to visit each of the widely dispersed sections of the ancient city. The best way to explore the site is to travel around it by a combination of light railway and horse-drawn carriage.

The Carthaginians

Remarkably little is known of the Carthaginians and their lifestyle, largely because no written works of theirs have

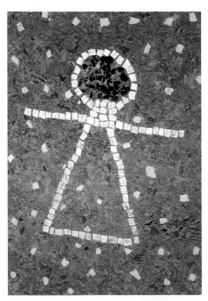

A mosaic of the Carthaginian goddess Tanit

ever been found. They were, above all, sharp commercial traders, like their Phoenician forebears, and were not considered to be great aesthetes or lovers of culture. From the relics that have been unearthed, it seems that their religious rituals included human sacrifice. Sacrifice of the first-born son was actually a practice widely followed throughout the Near East. The ceremonies were conducted by moonlight, and boys between the ages of two and twelve were sacrificed to the sun-god Baal Ammon and the moon goddess Tanit. Musicians and dancers wearing grotesque masks attended the ceremony, which is depicted in the Musée National de Carthage (National Archaeological Museum) on Byrsa Hill.

Priests carried the boys' bodies to the statues of the gods, where they were cremated. The ashes were placed in funerary urns, many of which can be seen about the site. The Tophet, the sanctuary where these sacrifices were made, is in the extreme south of the site, near Carthage-Salammbô station, close to the Punic harbours. The few artefacts that remain from Punic times, such as pottery and jewellery, show Syrian, Egyptian and Greek influences. *17km (10½ miles) east of Tunis. Open: daily 8am–7pm in summer, 8.30am–5pm in winter. Admission charge, with tickets available from three locations: the National Museum, the Thermes d'Antonin Pius (Antonine Baths) and the Villa de Volières.*

The Punic sanctuary of the Tophet

Dido and Aeneas

Carthage was the setting for one of the earliest classic tragic love stories, the story of conflict between personal feelings and public responsibilities.

It is in Books I and IV of Virgil's *Aeneid* that the story is told of Princess Dido's flight from the mighty Phoenician city of Tyre (in today's Lebanon) after her brother, King Pygmalion, had killed her husband Acerbas. Accompanied by a group of loyal followers, she set sail across the Mediterranean and landed on the north coast of Tunisia, where she asked the local Numidian ruler for as much land as could be contained within an ox hide, to which he agreed. Then, with typical Phoenician cunning, Dido cut the hide into very thin long strips, joined them together and encircled enough land on which to build the city of Kart Hadasht, where Carthage now stands.

The storm, prelude to the consummation of their passion

During the time of the construction of the city, Aeneas and a band of his followers – the sole survivors of the sack of Troy – were washed ashore nearby. Dido took Aeneas in and an affair developed, consummated out of doors to a backdrop of thunder and lightning and wailing nymphs. By allowing this to happen, Dido alienated not only the local Numidians by refusing to marry one of their kings, but also her own Phoenician followers, by failing to remain faithful to her dead husband.

When Aeneas announced that he must, in spite of his feelings for her, complete his destiny as predicted by Apollo's oracle in Lycia (southern Turkey), and sail for Italy to found a new Troy (Rome) for his people, Dido saw this as a heartless rejection and was sure that it would destroy her. She promised that she would haunt Aeneas with 'flames of blackest pitch' and proclaimed 'wherever you go my spectre will be there'.

After Aeneas left, Dido had herself burnt on a funeral pyre, an act symbolic of Carthage's future destruction at the hands of imperial Rome.

Dido inspects progress in the construction of Carthage

Gammarth

Known for its excellent fish restaurants and fine hotels, the fashionable beach resort of Gammarth lies at the end of the headland of Cap Carthage, where the road culminates in the Cap Carthage Méditerranée tourism project (*see map, p47*). The Abou Nawas Hotel here is one of the most beautiful coastal hotels in the country. On the Hauts de Gammarth above the beach you will find the French military cemetery where some 4,000 Frenchmen who were killed in World War II lie buried. *24km (15 miles) northeast of Tunis.*

Sidi Bou Said's most famous tea house, the Café des Nattes

La Goulette

The old walled town of La Goulette, once a corsair community with a large Jewish population, is now very run down (*see map, p47*). Due to its location at the point where the canal meets the sea (hence its name, The Gullet), the town is Tunis' outer harbour, so that most cargo ships bound for Tunis, along with passenger ferries from France, Sicily and Italy, pass through here. *15km (9 1/2 miles) northeast of Tunis.*

Lac de Tunis

Originally a series of shallow creeks, the Lake of Tunis (on which the city stands) was created in the 9th century by the Arabs, who dredged a 10km- (6-mile-) long canal between Tunis and the sea (*see map, p47*). Two harbours, one at each end of the canal, were built. Although the lake is little more than a brackish lagoon, it attracts flocks of flamingos and other long-legged wading birds, which feed here.

La Marsa

This is the most upmarket resort on the Bay of Tunis, and also where the TGM railway line ends (*see map, p47*). Stroll around its streets to admire the lavish villas and palaces of the wealthy, the finest of which are the British and French ambassadors' residences. It was the British ambassador who suggested to the *bey* in the 19th century that the railway causeway should be built to make his journey to the embassy easier. *22km (13 1/2 miles) northeast of Tunis.*

The long stretch of beach at La Marsa

Sidi Bou Said

This is without doubt the prettiest village in Tunisia, with its immaculate white houses, adorned with bright blue shutters and doors and wrought-iron window grilles (*see map, p47*). Its reputation was established when three young painters – Paul Klee, August Macke and Louis Moillet – stayed here in 1914 and painted a series of town scenes which were widely acclaimed. Even before then, it was known within Tunisia as an artists' village, when members of the Husseinite dynasty set up their court here in the 18th century.

Today the village enjoys a special protected status to prevent further development and, despite the number of tourists who invade it each summer,

Sidi Bou Said retains a calm and elegant atmosphere. It's almost compulsory for visitors to sit in the famous Café des Nattes, sipping mint tea and watching the chic and fashionable locals go by. The Dar Said Hotel, a converted palace with lovely gardens and pool, makes a very attractive, if expensive, alternative to Tunis as a base for exploring the north.

The town gets its name from a 13th-century Sufi (follower of a mystical form of Islam) who settled here after his pilgrimage to Mecca. His mosque and *zaouia* (Islamic religious school) are tucked away in the centre of town, but only Muslims are allowed inside.

20km (12 1/2 miles) northeast of Tunis.

Tour: Carthage

This excursion consists of a pleasant half-hour train ride from the centre of Tunis across the Lake of Tunis and out to the suburb of Carthage, then a ride in a horse-drawn carriage or a walk around the major sections of the archaeological site of Carthage. In the summer months, riding in the carriage gives visitors the advantage of shade from the sun.

Allow half a day. Start at the TGM railway station in Tunis.

1 Tunis

The station lies at the extreme eastern end of Avenue Habib Bourguiba. Buy your ticket and catch any train as all trains travel along the same line. The train runs along the spit of land that crosses the Lac de Tunis. To the right is the industrial and distinctly polluted port of Tunis.

Get off at the sixth station, Carthage-Hannibal, to begin your tour of the major sights.

2 Carthage-Hannibal

Here, from June through to September, you will find what are variously called calèches, hippomobiles or simply horse-drawn carriages. You must agree a price for the trip (a two-hour tour should cost about 8 dinars per carriage), then set off through the leafy, plush suburbs towards the Thermes d'Antonin Pius (Baths of Antoninus), where you buy your site entry ticket.

3 Thermes d'Antonin Pius

Set in their own archaeological park, these ruins are the most visually impressive in Carthage. The baths were the largest in the Roman Empire outside Rome, but all that remains today is the basement. The spectacular 15m- (49ft-) high single pillar

(re-erected), one of many that supported the roof of the baths, gives an idea of the scale of the complex. With a huge sunbathing terrace and an open-air swimming pool beside, the baths were the ancient equivalent of our modern leisure complexes, where the pleasure-loving Romans enjoyed socialising, exercising and pampering their bodies. The paths to the complex, which follow the streets of the old Roman city, are lined with Punic stelae and other architectural fragments. Adjacent to the site stands one of Habib Bourguiba's many presidential palaces. Don't take photographs even in the general direction of the palace as this is prohibited and likely to result in your immediate arrest.
Continue to Byrsa Hill.

4 Byrsa Hill

This was the centre of the original Punic city. Here you will find the Musée National de Carthage (National Archaeological Museum) and the Quartier Punique (Carthaginian Quarter), showing the layout of the early Punic houses (of the 4th century BC), with their circular underground cisterns. The imposing mock-Byzantine Cathédrale (Cathedral of Louis IX), which was built in 1890, dominates the hill. It is now deconsecrated but still open to the public, and from its terrace there is a splendid view over modern Carthage, the Punic harbour, La Goulette and Tunis.

From Byrsa Hill, get the calèche *to take you to the Parque Archéologique des Villas Romaines (Roman Villas Archaeological Park), which is next to the theatre and odeon.*

5 Parque Archéologique des Villas Romaines

The highlight here is the Villa de Volières, a restored house of the 3rd century AD. Its original floor mosaics survive, and give a vivid impression of the lavish lifestyle enjoyed by wealthy Romans.
Return to Carthage-Hannibal station.

The Quartier Punique on Byrsa Hill

The north

The landscapes of northern Tunisia are so different from what most people expect of North Africa that they could easily be mistaken for southern Europe. The Mejerda valley, with its green rolling hills, was once one of the great granaries for Rome, and the remains of the ancient cities of Bulla Regia, Chemtou and Utica are reminders of those days.

The French colonialists also recognised the farming potential here and used it for intensive crop production. After independence, Tunisians set up their own villages of houses with red-tiled roofs and whitewashed walls. These, along with wooden farmhouses and herds of cattle grazing on green slopes, give the Mejerda valley an almost alpine look. The wettest season here is between October and March, and rainfall in the valley and the surrounding mountains is three times heavier than in London. In winter the mountains are covered in snow.

North of the river, a limestone mountain chain, which is partially covered in thick oak forest, runs parallel with the coastline. The town of Aïn Draham, south of Tabarka, sits in the middle of such a forest, which today as in the past is popular for boar-hunting. There is a noticeable contrast between the indigenous Berber population of these mountain highlands, with their traditional lifestyles, and the more prosperous townspeople of the valley.

The coastline is mainly rocky, but has magnificent isolated sandy beaches like Sidi Ali el-Mekki and Raf Raf, both near Ghar el-Melh, Plage Zouiraa, near Tabarka, and Rass Engelah, near Bizerte.

The two principal resorts of the north coast are Bizerte and Tabarka. In the 16th, 17th and 18th centuries these towns were major trading ports, where Italian, Spanish and French ships would call. Their harbour fortresses bear testimony to the vigorous battles that were regularly fought to gain control of these two ports. Today the area is known as the Coral Coast since the warm waters of the Mediterranean allow coral to thrive, especially in the sea off Tabarka.

BIZERTE AND SURROUNDS
Bizerte

The second-largest town on the north coast after Tunis, Bizerte has developed into an attractive resort. Hotels along the Corniche (coast road) face out over dunes and uncrowded sandy beaches. Bizerte has been a major port since Phoenician times, and it was the Phoenicians who first dug the canal link from the inland Lac de Bizerte to the sea. Under Turkish rule in the 16th century, the town was a well-known pirates' den, and in the 19th century the French made it their chief naval base, only evacuating it in 1963. Tunisian forces then moved in, and it remains the country's major military base.

Bizerte's central tourist attraction today is the old harbour (Vieux Port), around which cluster the narrow streets of the old Arab médina, which has a

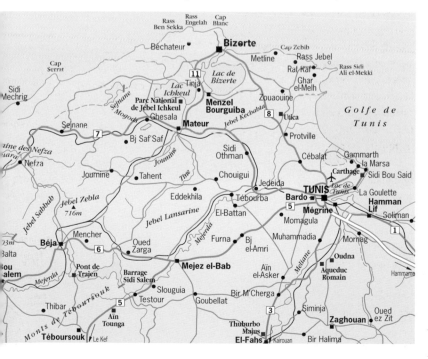

covered market and medieval forts redolent of its piratical past. The Sidi el-Hani fort houses a small oceanographic museum with a terrace café that enjoys a fine view over the old town.

65km (40 miles) northwest of Tunis.

Ghar el-Melh

The lagoon of Ghar el-Melh (meaning 'salt cave' in Arabic) was one of the main pirate lairs along the Barbary Coast. Today the shallow lagoon is all but cut off from the sea as a result of the silting up of the Mejerda estuary. It was in this bay in 1535 that the Holy Roman Emperor Charles V prepared his vast army for the great siege of Tunis. The village that remains has three impressive forts, which are used as workshops, boatyards and National Guard premises.

35km (21½ miles) east of Bizerte.

Raf Raf

Raf Raf is famous for its crescent-shaped beach of fine sand. It faces the barren island of Pilau and, although it is attractive from a distance, the sand is often blighted by seaweed and litter. The women still wear traditional dress, and the local embroidery is well known.

38km (23½ miles) east of Bizerte.

Rass Engelah

Rass Engelah is an excellent long sandy beach on a headland west of Bizerte. Béchateur is the nearest village.

16km (10 miles) west of Bizerte.

The fine sand beach of Raf Raf

Mosaic floor of a Roman villa, Utica

Rass Sidi Ali el-Mekki

This is possibly the loveliest beach in Tunisia, and its relative inaccessibility means that even in the height of summer it is quiet, with only a few straw huts and a handful of cafés. The beach is named after the tomb of Sidi Ali el-Mekki, a fortress-like edifice on the headland above.

6km (3½ miles) east of Ghar el-Melh.

Utica

An ancient Phoenician settlement, Utica became an important Roman port. It has been only partially excavated because it was buried under 5m (16ft) of alluvial mud from the Mejerda river. Today Utica lies about 15km (9½ miles) from the sea.

The best-preserved of the ruins that have been uncovered are the Roman baths and the Maison de la Cascade (House of the Waterfall), a Roman villa with a fine mosaic floor. Note

the unusual Punic cemetery of the 6th century BC.

35km (21½ miles) southeast of Bizerte, 37km (22 miles) north of Tunis.

Aïn Draham

This small town, unique in Tunisia and indeed in North Africa, looks as if it has been transplanted straight from the foothills of the Alps. The surrounding mountains are green with ferns and moss-covered cork trees, and rich in forest wildlife. Unfortunately, the wildlife here is unprotected and is being hunted to extinction. Hare, jackal, fox, wildcat and boar still inhabit the mountains, but the last lions and leopards were shot in the 1920s and 1930s. There is good two- and three-star accommodation for the few tourists who venture here, many using it as a base for walks along the waymarked mountain paths.

25km (15½ miles) south of Tabarka, on the Jendouba road.

Bizerte's picturesque old harbour was once a pirate headquarters

Béja

Throughout its history Béja has been the chief town of the fertile Mejerda plain. It was the centre of the Roman granary and is the heart of Tunisia's lucrative corn market today. Béja's interest for tourists lies in the old médina sandwiched in the middle of the new town. The Byzantine *kasbah* (fortress) is a garrison barracks (not open to the public).
109km (68 miles) west of Tunis.

Bulla Regia

With an attractive rural setting on a gentle hillside sloping down towards the Mejerda valley, Bulla Regia was one of the wealthiest cities in Roman Africa. Today, famous for its underground villas with beautiful mosaic floors, it is one of the most remarkable Roman sites in the world. The remains of baths, temples, basilicas, a theatre and a forum can also be seen here.

The merchants who grew rich from trading in corn and olives built their sumptuous villas underground for protection both from the heat of summer and the cold of winter. Many of the villas have a central courtyard with pillars, reached by an open stone staircase, and several rooms off the courtyard, with many fine mosaic floors dating from the 3rd and 4th centuries. Most of the best mosaics have been removed to the Musée du Bardo in Tunis, but a few remain *in situ*, notably that in the Maison d'Amphitrite (House of Amphitrite),

A loo for two – part of the bath complex at Bulla Regia

which shows Venus, Marina and Neptune riding a marine centaur.

Other impressive villas at Bulla Regia are the Maison de la Chasse (House of the Hunt) and the Maison de la Pêche (House of the Fishing Scene), which has a mosaic showing a sea full of fish being caught by cupids and ducks.
6km (3½ miles) north of Jendouba, 60km (37 miles) south of Tabarka. Open: 8am–6pm daily. Admission charge.

Chemtou (Thuburnica)

Set in a beautiful rural landscape of rolling green hills, Chemtou (ancient Roman Simitthus) was once famous for its marble quarries. The largest in North Africa, these quarries yielded a fine dark yellow marble with heavy veining, known as *antico giallo*. After purple porphyry from Egypt and green serpentine from Sparta, *antico giallo* ranked third in the Roman Empire as the most precious stone in the world. Today on the hillsides beside the quarries you can view the ruins of the slaves' work camp, baths and a theatre. *28km (17¹/₂ miles) northwest of Jendouba, off the Tabarka road. Site always open. Free.*

Tabarka

Close to the Algerian border, Tabarka feels rather like a French Mediterranean town, with its neat red-roofed houses set in tree-lined avenues and hills rising up behind. Sandy beaches extend to the east, while to the west are myriad small rocky coves. With only a handful of hotels and restaurants, Tabarka makes a tranquil base for a holiday.

The chief monument here is the fine Genoese fort on the hill that is now joined to the mainland by a causeway. The museum was once housed in the old basilica, originally a Roman cistern, but has now been transferred to the fort. At the end of Avenue Habib Bourguiba is the much-photographed rock formation called Les Aiguilles (The Needles), pinnacles of rock that rise dramatically on the shoreline.

East of Tabarka, on the Nefza road, a tarmacked road heads through pine forest for some 13km (8 miles) to reach Plage Zouiraa, a beautiful long sandy beach backed by dunes. The coral reef off Tabarka is impressive and this is a popular diving-holiday resort. *136km (85 miles) southwest of Bizerte, 175km (109 miles) west of Tunis.*

The north

The Genoese fort at Tabarka dominates the former pirate harbour, now used only by fishermen

Drive: Jebel Ichkeul National Park

This drive from Bizerte to one of Tunisia's national parks makes an unusual outing. Set on the shores of Lac Ichkeul, below Mount Ichkeul, Jebel Ichkeul National Park is a haven for fish, wildlife and, above all, birds. In fact, the park is the most important bird and wildlife sanctuary in North Africa. As facilities en route are minimal, it is best to take your own picnic.

Allow half a day.

Leaving Bizerte on the Mateur road, the route passes Bizerte airport and skirts Lac de Bizerte (Lake Bizerte).

1 Lac de Bizerte

Although it is marred by military installations and belching factories, Lac de Bizerte plays a vital part in the ecology of Lac Ichkeul, to which it is joined by the Oued Tinja, a shallow river.

2 Tinja

The village of Tinja straddles the river. Here you will see hundreds of nets for catching eel and mullet as they pass from Lac Ichkeul out towards the sea. The river also has a complicated system of dams, which are designed to counteract the effect of other dams and therefore to keep the water level sufficiently high. Water levels at Lac Ichkeul are sometimes so low as to threaten its viability. The reason for this is that other dams on the lake's feeder rivers are depriving it of more and more water which is needed to supply tourist complexes and irrigation projects.

About 5km (3 miles) beyond Tinja on the Mateur road, a right fork leads to Jebel Ichkeul National Park.

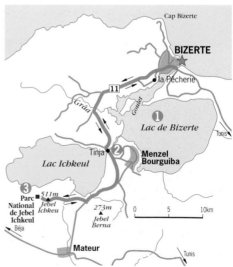

3 Parc National de Jebel Ichkeul

In the marshland to your right look out for water buffalo, introduced to the marshes in 1729. Down to just three females in 1963 after excessive hunting, they are now gaining in numbers through a breeding programme. The gravel road passes a quarry at the foot of Jebel Ichkeul, where there are a few clusters of simple stone huts roofed with marshland reed. The people here work the quarries and are allowed to keep their own sheep and cows; the animals are often penned into thorn-bush enclosures, which double as washing lines for the colourful clothes of the women.

The road climbs up a wooded ridge on a peninsula to end at the Ecology Museum, which gives a fascinating account of the park's birds and other wildlife. Beside the museum is an excellent viewing point over the lake. This is a vast expanse, fringed by reeds, on which huge numbers of aquatic birds can be seen. The lake is too shallow to be navigable, and the low water level in recent years has meant that salt water from Lac de Bizerte has been flowing in, threatening the freshwater plants on which the lake's sensitive ecology depends. The lake is used by around 150,000 waterfowl, which winter here after their migration from eastern Europe. Peak occupancy is from October to February, although a few stay until spring. From the museum a track leads towards the shoreline north of the mountain where there are more viewing points.

Jebel Ichkeul, an impressive limestone mountain, rises to a height of 511m (1,677 ft) on the south side of the lake. As early as the 13th century it was a royal hunting park. Boar and jackal are the main surviving wildlife here, along with otters, tortoises, porcupines and mongooses. Various tracks lead over the mountain, and with careful navigation you can explore them and return to the museum.

The tranquil lake at Jebel Ichkeul

Drive: Jebel Ichkeul National Park

Cap Bon and Hammamet

The Cap Bon may as well be still joined to Sicily. Citrus groves and vineyards dominate the Garden of Tunisia. The blue médina of Hammamet leaves you in no doubt though that you are in the Arab world.

CAP BON

Cap Bon is the peninsula at the northern tip of Tunisia, which aeons ago was connected to Sicily and southern Italy. In many ways Cap Bon has more of a southern European than a North African atmosphere. With landscapes of vineyards, citrus groves and rolling green fields, its nickname is the Garden of Tunisia.

Historically, the peninsula has tended to be peripheral to the main dramas that were played out between the northern and the eastern coastal regions, and it is still something of a backwater. A circuit of Cap Bon from Hammamet takes about seven hours. Besides the scenery, the main features of interest here are Kelibia and its castle, the Punic ruins at Kerkouane, the caves and Roman quarry of El-Haouaria and finally the spa and springs of Korbous.

Travelling by public transport, you would need to allow two days for a circuit of Cap Bon, and even then be prepared for a lot of walking as all the main sites lie off the major routes. Further south, the beach between Hammamet and Nabeul, with its fine white sand, is one of the finest in the country. It marks the divide between Cap Bon and Tunisia's eastern coastal plain, which stretches away southward to Sfax and beyond. The stability and long-term habitation of the area is based on the fertility of the hinterland, which is so intensively planted with olive groves that it is known as the Olive Coast.

The eastern coastline, known as the Sahel (Arabic for 'coast'), boasts many fine long sandy beaches. This is naturally where the resorts have tended to build up, the main ones being Monastir, Port El-Kantaoui and Sousse. Sousse and Sfax are both busy commercial cities, but retain at their heart old walled médinas with some of Tunisia's finest early Islamic architecture. Mahdia is a sleepier fishing town with a less developed resort. Sousse's beaches are at nearby Skanès and Port El-Kantaoui. Sfax has no beaches at all, so sand- and sea-lovers head for the blissfully tranquil Îles Kerkennah (Kerkennah Islands), a short distance offshore.

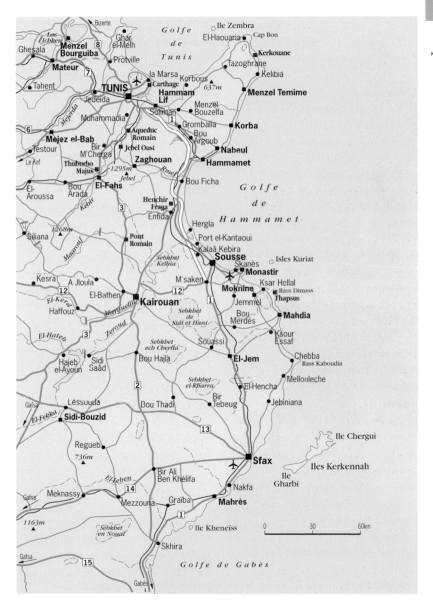

A short distance inland from the coastal plain are two of Tunisia's most memorable sites – the colossal Roman amphitheatre at El-Jem, and the holy city of Kairouan, where Tunisia's largest concentration of important Islamic monuments is to be found.

El-Haouaria

El-Haouaria is famous for its Roman quarry caves, right at the sea's edge. The best way to reach them is to follow signs for the Restaurant des Grottes, which take you straight through the town and out at the other side, to a hill overlooking the sea. The setting is dramatic, with the strikingly mountainous island of Zembra directly opposite and waves crashing against the rocks below.

Altogether there are 24 quarry caves. The most surprising thing about them

Dramatic caves of the Roman quarry at El-Haouaria

is the orangish-brown colour of the limestone rock, which was used for decorative carving throughout the Roman and Byzantine world. Like all mines and quarries in Roman times, they were worked by slaves, many of whom would have been Christians. El-Haouaria is also known for its falconry festival (*see p156*).

14km (8½ miles) northwest of Kerkouane, 93km (58 miles) north of Hammamet. Caves open: daily 8am–6pm. Admission charge.

Kelibia

On reaching Kelibia follow the signs to 'Port' and 'Plage' until you see the castle looming up on the left. An unsignposted chalky track leads to the castle gates, from which a short walk takes you through the mighty entrance. In the far right-hand corner is an underground prison, where a vertical iron-rung ladder gives access to five interconnecting cells. The castle walls date from the 6th-century Byzantine period and you can walk round the ramparts for fine views in all directions.

11km (6½ miles) south of Kerkouane, 68km (42 miles) northeast of Hammamet. Castle open: daily 8am–6pm. Admission charge.

Kerkouane

Kerkouane, discovered only in 1952, is Tunisia's most impressive Carthaginian site. More vividly than any other of the Carthaginian ruins in Tunis it gives an insight into the lifestyle of the people who lived here in the 4th century BC.

Set right on the sea, the site makes a good picnic spot, although the shoreline is too rocky for swimming. The whole site is beautifully tended, with colourful gardens lining the approach path, and the sign of the simple triangular-bodied goddess Tanit drawn by flowers. The site also has a museum, well laid-out with Carthaginian objects from all over Tunisia. Notice especially the lovely jewellery and the delicately carved blue and yellow pottery. There are no refreshments on the site.

In the knee-high ruins of the compact houses that remain, there are bathrooms made from pink cement and one cluster of larger houses has pretty mosaic flooring with the figure of the goddess Tanit in white at the threshold. It is estimated that around 2,500 people – many of them fishermen, stonemasons, ironworkers, glass-blowers or sculptors – lived here. *14km (8¹/₂ miles) south of El-Haouaria, 79km (49 miles) northeast of Hammamet. Site open: daily 9am–4.30pm in winter, 9am–7pm in summer. Admission charge.*

Korbous

The most striking aspect of the spa town of Korbous is its dramatic approach. The drive from El-Haouaria to Korbous passes through open countryside and culminates in a steep descent to the shoreline, where just before the spa town itself a hot sulphurous spring called Aïn el-Atrous gushes out into the sea. The springs

A view of the spa resort of Korbous

Steps lead up to the entrance of the *kasbah* at Hammamet

here and in the town itself were popular even in Roman times. Sandwiched in a little gully, the pretty whitewashed houses have a Moorish appearance and the town has an appealing, relaxed atmosphere.
60km (37 miles) north of Hammamet, 55km (34 miles) southwest of El-Haouaria.

Nabeul

Nabeul's main claim to fame is its exquisite pottery and what passes for its Friday camel market. Like Hammamet, Nabeul has good sandy beaches lined with hotels, but its town, set a little way inland, is dusty and commercial with no médina or *kasbah*. Most people come to Nabeul simply to shop.

The town's sights are restricted to a small archaeological museum and a minor Roman site. The museum has some fine 2,500-year-old Carthaginian statues and other sculptures, and some striking courtyard mosaics, most notably of Bacchus, god of wine, riding on a leopard's back. The Roman site, known as Neapolis, was discovered when the first tourist hotel (now called the Aquarius) was being built on the beach. Faint traces of a palace, its courtyard and dining room remain, but the ruins are confusing and not well maintained, so they are of no great interest to visitors.

Every Friday morning, Nabeul hosts a famous 'camel market'. The main street is closed to traffic to allow hundreds of local people and coach-loads of tourists, but only a few camels, to mingle for a chaotic few hours. Most camels here, however, are of the soft-toy variety.

Nabeul's pottery dates back to the 16th century, when the high-quality Cap Bon clay was first exploited. The elaborately coloured pottery makes excellent souvenirs.
Museum. Avenue Habib Bourguiba. Open: Tue–Sun 9am–4.30pm. Admission charge. 10km (6 miles) northeast of Hammamet.

Hammamet

Despite the invasion of package tourists that keeps this resort busy from May through to October, Hammamet remains a remarkably pleasant and relaxing place. Its centre, set on the edge of the beautiful sandy bay, is a typically Tunisian medieval walled médina. But what makes Hammamet stand out above the other resorts of the coastal plain is its cleanliness. It has none of the scruffiness and litter of other médinas, like Sousse and

Hammamet

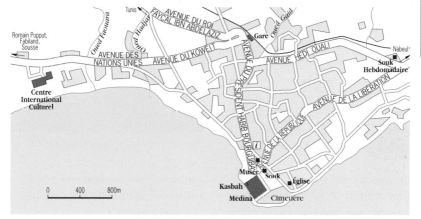

Kairouan, and no unsavoury odours assail the nostrils as you tread the back streets. With whitewashed houses with blue shuttered windows and flowers tumbling freely over garden walls, everything here is immaculate.

The médina and *kasbah*

The médina and *kasbah* sit on the headland that separates the beach areas into north and south Hammamet. There is usually a certain amount of hustle and bustle along the promenade and round the foot of the *kasbah*, but the moment you step through one of the médina's huge 15th-century gates, you enter a world where the pace of life is different. Although the first streets you come to are lined with souvenir stalls, the atmosphere is not pushy and unpleasant, and there are ample opportunities for souvenir shopping. Beyond these streets, the shops give way to whitewashed houses either side of delightfully quiet alleyways. Many of

the doors here are decorated with talismanic fishes or with the ubiquitous Hand of Fatima (the Prophet Muhammad's daughter). Opposite the Great Mosque, look out for the green-and-white-striped door that marks the entrance to the public Turkish baths (men in the mornings and women in the afternoons). The restored 15th-century minaret of the Great Mosque is

The minaret of Hammamet's Great Mosque

a good landmark to keep in sight when you are wandering around the médina.

The *kasbah* (fort) itself is in the corner of the médina closest to the sea. A colossal ramp leads up to the entrance and inside is an attractive courtyard with a few cannon balls and architectural fragments scattered about. The main reason for visiting the *kasbah* is to take in the view from the wide wall walk, which is still intact all the way round the ramparts and which offers tantalising glimpses into the houses of the médina, across the bay and out to sea.
Kasbah. Open: daily 8am–9pm in summer, 8.30am–6pm in winter. Admission charge.

Beaches

The sandy beaches lining the coast on either side of Hammamet are among the best in the country, and are made even more attractive by the distant hills inland, which give some relief and contour to the beach vistas. The beaches to the south of the resort are generally more sheltered than those to the north, which is worth bearing in mind during the windy spring months. All the beach hotels are built along the lines of palm trees and, in keeping with planning restrictions, do not rise above the height of the trees. Their gardens often give direct access to the beach, but while each hotel claims exclusive rights, in practice every beach runs into the next and there is no way to prevent beach touts walking the full length of

The exotic pool at the Cultural Centre

the beaches in front of the 40-odd hotels, exploiting to the full their chances of selling to tourists.

Fabiland

About 6km (3¹/₂ miles) south of Hammamet town centre, close to the Hotel Safir and Hotel Kerkouane, Fabiland is a good distraction from the beach for children aged between eight and fifteen, with a funfair, rides and slot machines.
70km (43 miles) southeast of Tunis, 16km (10 miles) southwest of Nabeul. Open: daily 9.30am–6.30pm in season.

Centre International Culturel

The guardian at the gate here will let you in at any time during daylight hours, unless a conference is in progress, so if you get the chance, seize it, for this is surely one of the most idyllic and romantic places in the world. Built by a Romanian millionaire called George Sebastian in the 1920s, this is a lavish white villa in a simple yet sybaritic style. Other wealthy European and American expatriates followed suit and soon a small colony of art-lovers were living in the bay. Most of their villas have been incorporated into the larger beach hotels.

The great American architect Frank Lloyd Wright called this villa 'the most beautiful house I know'. Less distinguished critics, however, often leave wondering why he was so enthusiastic. During the 1920s it became a fashionable meeting place and among people entertained here were the painter Paul Klee and the writer André Gide. During World War II, Field Marshal Rommel stayed here briefly, to be followed by British prime ministers Winston Churchill and Anthony Eden. The villa, now state property, is used to host the annual summer festival of music and drama in July and August, as well as for cultural conferences.

The villa is not large, but each room is immaculately designed, with a recurring decorative theme of black and white. In the downstairs bedroom the showpiece is the splendid sunken bath for four, its shape modelled on early Christian fonts, while the toilet and basin are hidden away in mirrored closets. Upstairs, one of the bedrooms has a shaded terrace lined with bamboo. The gardens, full of little paths leading to follies and hidden dens, are also a delight to explore. The café here is a very pleasant place to have a coffee.

2km (1¹/₄ miles) from the town centre. Avenue des Nations Unies. Usually open during office hours unless a conference is in progress (ask at the tourist information office). Admission charge.

Pupput

This Roman site is unremarkable as it is in a state of considerable disrepair and there is very little to see. It is only of real interest to those with a strong interest in archaeology and a good imagination. The mosaics are very faded.

On the Sousse road, 6km (3¹/₂ miles) southwest of the centre of Hammamet. Open: daily 8am–sunset. Admission charge.

Oued Faouara

Either your hotel or the tourist office will arrange a half-day excursion, on horseback or by horse-drawn carriage, to this peaceful dry riverbed, inland near Bir Bou Regba. The goal of the outing is a small waterfall several kilometres up the riverbed, where the spring-fed stream runs over some old Roman stones, thought to be the beginning of an aqueduct. The round trip takes three to four hours. It is possible to make the trip by car, taking just half an hour to reach the waterfall, but you need a guide or very detailed instructions to show you the way.

A good-luck fish tile on a house in the médina

Drive: Hammamet to Thuburbo Majus

A relaxed day trip from Hammamet, with fine scenery, this drive takes in the charming town of Zaghouan and the superb Roman ruins of Thuburbo Majus.

Allow 4 to 6 hours, including time for a picnic.

1 Hammamet

Leave Hammamet on the main road to Tunis. At the junction with the motorway, where the sign to Tunis points to the right, follow the sign to Hammam Jedidi, which points straight over the top of the motorway. It is route 28 on your map. The road is very quiet and the tranquillity of the attractive landscape is a welcome respite from the bustle of the coast. Straight ahead is the imposing hill-mountain of Jebel Zaghouan.

2 Zaghouan

Below the mountain the unspoilt town of Zaghouan enjoys an almost alpine setting, its red-roofed houses standing out against the green of the forested slopes. Follow the signs to 'Centre Ville' and then take the left fork marked 'Hôtel des Nymphes'. The steep, narrow cobbled streets are charming and water is abundant as Zaghouan is famous for its mountain springs. The road ends at the Nymphaeum, a Roman water temple beside a pleasant café. The Nymphaeum

was built by the Emperor Hadrian in the 2nd century AD, to mark the head of a stream that, running from here, and on via an astonishing aqueduct, supplied Carthage with fresh water.

If you decide to explore more of the countryside around Zaghouan, you can cut short your drive and just enjoy walking on the hillside or even climb the 3km (2-mile) track to the summit of Jebel Zaghouan 1,295m (4,249ft).

3 Jebel Zaghouan

The bird life, as well as the plants and trees, are plentiful here, and the atmosphere delightfully different from that of Hammamet.

To continue, follow the signs to Tunis out of Zaghouan on route 28, and after 4km (2½ miles) take the fork marked El-Fahs. Thuburbo Majus is signposted up a small 1km (⅔-mile) road to the left.

4 Thuburbo Majus

There are no facilities at the site, but it is an excellent picnic spot.

From Thuburbo Majus follow the main road north to Tunis (route 3), through pretty countryside, where a few decaying French colonial farm mansions can be seen. Soon after a fork in the road leading back to Zaghouan, you will see the unmistakable arches of an aqueduct.

5 Aqueduc Romain

Amazingly well preserved, considering its remarkable age and length, this is the remains of the Zaghouan–Carthage aqueduct. The road goes right through the aqueduct, and you can drive alongside it to the point where it crosses a railway line. You can even climb up inside and walk through the tunnel in which the water once flowed. *Continue to Muhammadia along route 3.*

6 Muhammadia

Here you can see further stretches of the aqueduct, as well as the huge bulk of a ruined 19th-century palace, its crumbling brickwork rising above the houses on top of the hill to the left.

Returning towards Hammamet on Autoroute 1, you pass the distinctive Jebel Bou Kornine (Two-Horned Mountain) on your left. It was once the sacred mountain of Carthage, but you will see its summit is now covered with masts and radio antennae.

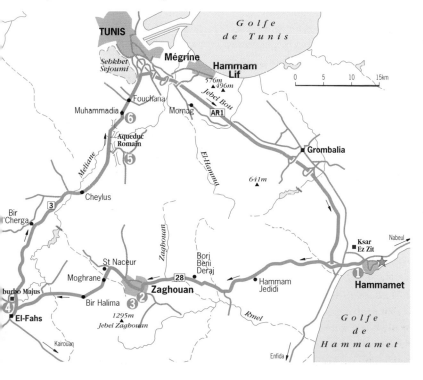

The Sahel

The central coast of Tunisia (sahel means 'shore' in Arabic) is where tourists congregate. Most of the resort areas are concentrated just outside the towns to preserve their ancient médina interiors.

MAHDIA

The prettiest place on the Sahel coast, Mahdia is a charming, typically Tunisian town with a fishing harbour and an ancient walled médina. Despite its excellent white sandy beach, Mahdia has been spared the attentions of developers and so remains remarkably unspoilt.

The médina

The entrance to the old town is through the heavily fortified gateway known as the Skifa el-Kahla (Dark Gate). This tunnel-like passageway is all that remains of the médina's 10th-century fortifications, which originally had six portcullises and a wrought-iron gate. The médina is quite small in comparison with other towns, but it has a maritime atmosphere quite unlike that of Tunis or the other cities of the Sahel. There are many workshops in the médina, and the weavers here are happy to talk about their work and demonstrate their craft.

Grande Mosquée (Great Mosque)

This remarkably plain structure, with no minaret, is actually a modern replica of the original 10th-century Fatimid mosque. The two bastions on the corners of the north wall were rainwater cisterns and the monumental entrance was for use only by the Fatimid caliph and his entourage.
Rue du Fort. Closed to non-Muslims.

North Africa's most magnificent Roman site, the amphitheatre at El-Jem

Borj el-Kebir (Great Tower)

Beyond the mosque the road leads through a cemetery on the rocky headland, out towards the lighthouse, to reach the large 16th-century Turkish fort. It houses various architectural fragments and some fine cannons, but the chief attraction is the view from its ramparts across the town and down to the old Fatimid rock-cut port below, now with a few fishing boats bobbing up and down.

Rue du Fort. Open: Mon–Sat 8am–noon, 2–6pm. Admission charge.
67km (42 miles) southeast of Sousse.

El-Jem

This magnificent amphitheatre, built around AD 200–300, is the most spectacular Roman site in North Africa. In a better state of preservation than the Coliseum in Rome, it is 149m (163yds) long and 24m (26yds) wide, and with seating rising in tiers to a height of 36m (118ft), it could hold some 30,000–35,000 spectators. Its location, apparently in complete isolation from any town, was connected to the great olive plantations of the Sahel. In Roman times, fortunes were made from the foreign trade in olive oil. As Thysdrus (the Roman name for El-Jem) rapidly developed, an amphitheatre was built for its inhabitants. The 'amusements' here were unimaginably bloodthirsty; when the killing of wild animals and gladiatorial combat had ceased to thrill, Christians, prisoners of war, slaves and

The entrance to the médina in Mahdia

criminals were thrown to starving lions instead. You can descend into the dark tunnel and see the cave-like rooms in which the victims were held before being either hauled up in cages or marched up the stairs at sword-point, into the blinding white light, to the roar of the crowd and a grisly death. Your ticket also gives you entrance to the charming small museum, adjacent to the Roman villa excavations, where some fine mosaics are displayed.

63km (39 miles) south of Sousse, 60km (37 miles) southeast of Kairouan.
Museum on Sfax road, 500m (550yds) south of the amphitheatre.
Amphitheatre. Open: daily 8.30am–6pm. Admission charge – includes museum (same opening hours).

Walk: Mahdia

This is probably the quietest and most relaxing walk you can enjoy in an urban setting in all of Tunisia, exploring a small town that is very accessible to visitors but not yet disturbed by tourism.

Allow 1½ to 2 hours.

1 Harbour

Begin your stroll on the promenade in front of the harbour. This is one of Tunisia's most important fishing ports, crammed with colourful wooden fishing boats that are laden with nets and traditional equipment. Lining the street opposite are Mahdia's smartest fish restaurants, which are well frequented by local people, especially on a Friday night.

About 100m (110yds) further on, beside the bus station, is the fish market.

2 Souk

This is a fascinating and lively affair, though make sure you are wearing footwear you do not mind getting smelly. On Fridays, the weekly food and goods market takes place beside the fish market, adding yet more bustle and colour.

Walk on to the main square and cross over to enter the médina by the huge gateway known as Skifa el-Kahla (Dark Passage).

3 Skifa el-Kahla

The Dark Passage was originally the only entrance to the walled Fatimid palace. On the right are the steps that climb from the tunnel to the top of the walls, which command fine views from the bastions.

Once out of the passageway bear slightly left to pass the tourist office and the Silk Museum (now closed) and 100m (110yds) further on, you come to Place du Claire. Skifa el-Kahla steps. Open: Mon–Sat 8am–noon, 2–6pm. Admission charge.

4 Place du Claire

Here you can stop to enjoy a coffee or tea at the little café opposite the Mosquée Mustapha Hamza.

Continue straight along the road to the next square, which faces the Grande Mosquée.

5 Grande Mosquée

This is a replica of the 10th-century Fatimid mosque that originally stood on this site, and which was blown up by the Spanish.

Beyond the Great Mosque, stroll out along the narrow coast road towards Borj el-Kebir (Great Tower). On the left of the road, just before the tower, you will pass the scant remains of the Mahdi's palace, which have been excavated.

6 Borj el-Kebir

There are great views from the top of this tower.

From the tower onwards, the rocky headland is picturesquely covered in a Muslim cemetery (the Cimetière).

7 Cimetière

Here local families may be seen picnicking on the tombstones of their dear departed. Notice the curved

indentation in the rocky shoreline where a few boats are still moored. This was the ancient Fatimid port, originally closed off by a chain suspended between two small towers at each end of the curve.

Right out on the headland is the Phare (Lighthouse).

8 Phare

This attractive working lighthouse is built on the site of a Fatimid tower. Nearby are some Phoenician rock-cut tombs. Complete the circuit now by walking along the coast road on the far side of the headland, along Rue Cap d'Africa. The houses in the médina are interesting and there are excellent views, especially at sunset, across to the sandy beaches where Mahdia's best hotels are to be found.

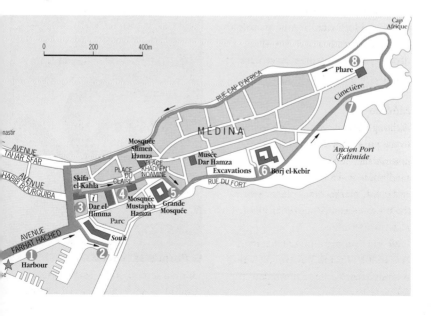

Monastir

Monastir has been almost overwhelmed by tourism. This means that, although it lacks character, it is generally cleaner and easier to navigate than other Tunisian towns. It also has a wide selection of hotels, restaurants and cafés. The beach hotels are mainly in Skanès, and while there is a sandy town beach, it is rather too public for most tourists, attracting an audience of curious local youths.

Bourguiba family mausoleum

Habib Bourguiba, the father of modern Tunisia, was born in Monastir in 1903. His lavish family mausoleum lies just north of the *ribat*. Grandiose in the extreme, the ensemble is instantly recognisable by its large golden dome. It is surrounded by the extensive cemetery of Sidi el-Mazeri, through which a processional avenue leading to the mausoleum has been cut. It is usually possible to enter the cemetery and look around the grounds.

Médina

Although heavily restored and sanitised to the point that it bears little resemblance to the more authentic médinas at Sousse, Kairouan and elsewhere, this médina offers visitors the pleasant experience of strolling along whitewashed alleys lined with craft and souvenir shops. The grand Bourguiba Mosque, built in 1963 and with fine marble steps, dominates the front of the médina.

Ribat of Harthema

This massive warren of rooms, towers, stairs and corridors is arranged on three levels and can take a good hour to

The mausoleum of the Bourguiba family is set in spacious grounds on the edge of Monastir

Climb the tower for spectacular views over the sea and the town. Adjoining the tower is the Great Mosque, with a square minaret. The *ribat* was built into the mosque's outer walls, and its residents would walk through the southern gate and straight into the mosque's prayer hall. From the tower you will also see a second large *ribat*, whose round towers and gatehouse have been well restored. Now converted, it is known as the Zaouia of Sidi Douib.

25km (15¹/₂ miles) southeast of Sousse. Route de la Corniche. Open: daily 9.30am–7pm in winter; 8am–7pm in summer. Admission charge.

Monastir's famous *ribat*

explore. It was built in AD 796 to defend the coast and the interior from attack by Sicilians, Vikings and other marauders, and against Berber raids. The current structure has been reworked many times since then. The *ribat* has been much favoured as a film location (from biblical epics like Zeffirelli's *The Life of Christ* to *Monty Python's Life of Brian*), and at times when filming is going on it is closed to the public. On one side of the courtyard is a prayer hall, now used as a museum where Islamic artefacts from all over the world are displayed. Note especially the Coptic (Egyptian Christian) weaving, Persian and Mughal miniatures, and gold jewellery.

Skanès

Skanès, Monastir's beach resort, has little else other than rows of tourist hotels set in the palm gardens that fringe its sandy beach. Skanès is one of Tunisia's more family-oriented resorts. Monastir airport is very close by.

5km (3 miles) west of Monastir.

RIBATS

A *ribat* is a fortified monastery. In the 8th and 9th centuries a chain of *ribats* was built along the Tunisian coast to protect the ruling Muslims against Berber raiders from the interior and Christian or pagan attacks from the sea. The soldiers who defended the *ribats* were volunteer monks (*murabitun*), for whom such service guaranteed a place in paradise. The central feature of a *ribat* is an open courtyard surrounded by small cells where the warrior-monks slept.

PORT EL-KANTAOUI

Port el-Kantaoui is a massive tourist complex (really a town with no traditional centre) just north of Sousse. It has been built up around a large and well-equipped marina, and there is a lively atmosphere around the médina. This is the resort that evokes most pride in Tunisians and they show it off with panache. It is the most Mediterranean of all Tunisian towns, and with its Andalucian architecture you could be in Spain were it not for the Arab tourists all around.

The name 'Kantaoui' means 'may everything go well' and all the facilities here are of a standard that will ensure your stay will satisfy you. In fact, some tourists come here and don't leave for the duration of their holiday. The only thing about el-Kantaoui is that it is not very Tunisian and if you stay here you won't get a flavour of the country at all. Some visitors may also find the atmosphere a little sterile.

The marina is filled with luxury yachts and cruise vessels. It is becoming a favourite spot with the Mediterranean yachting set, especially in the winter when the mooring fees here are considerably cheaper than in Europe.

The hotels, some of which are located on the sandy beaches either side of el-Kantaoui, have unashamedly modern, sometimes almost futuristic, exteriors. The whole tourist complex, featuring accommodation, restaurants, cafés and expensive boutique-style shops, has been designed in a modern yet traditional style, with narrow lanes and arches among the dazzling white buildings. El-Kantaoui is a very smart place and, for those who might find it difficult to acclimatise to the exotic nature of Arab society, this town should provide a gentle introduction. It is also an ideal base from which to explore and make daytrips.

11km (7 miles) north of Sousse.

Port el-Kantaoui's fashionable marina lives by night as well as day

Habib Bourguiba – Father of the Nation

Throughout North Africa the name Habib Bourguiba is synonymous with modern Tunisia. This inspirational leader ruled the country from its independence in 1956 until 1987. Born in 1903, into a lower-middle-class family from Monastir, Bourguiba won a scholarship to study in Tunis, then in Paris. He became a lawyer and returned to Tunis in 1927. His political ambitions were then aroused, and he published a nationalist newspaper that criticised the French administration. In 1934, he founded the Neo-Destour Party, a radical group that broke away from the mainstream nationalist Destour Party, which was dominated by intellectual élitists.

With his character and background, Bourguiba enjoyed a unique popularity. Recognising the potential threat that he posed, the French banned his party and arrested him. During the 1930s and 1940s, the struggle for Tunisian independence continued, and Bourguiba was arrested. Undaunted, he continued the struggle. Eventually, due to the strength of support from ordinary Tunisians and mounting unrest, the French conceded that Bourguiba should lead Tunisia to independence.

On becoming president in 1956, Bourguiba instituted elections to the National Assembly, which in turn gave him sweeping powers. He introduced social reforms that gave women greater equality, encouraged education for all, improved healthcare and reduced the power of religious authorities. This benign dictatorship created stability but not prosperity. When unrest broke out, Bourguiba repressed it harshly and his censorship of all opposition brought him much criticism.

As Bourguiba's mental health deteriorated, he suffered depression and dementia. He also showed lack of judgement in politics. This eventually paralysed the government, and in 1987, aged 84, he was removed from office by a coup. It was a sad end for Tunisia's great statesman. There were rumours that his successor, Ben Ali, had him under house arrest. Bourguiba died in April 2000, and was buried quietly. Many felt he deserved a state funeral, but that it was denied for political reasons.

Sousse

Tunisia's third-largest city after Tunis and Sfax, Sousse is an unusual combination of beach resort, industrial port and ancient Islamic city. Each part of Sousse is separate, and the beach is 10 minutes' walk from the old médina. Passing from one world to the other so quickly and so completely adds enormously to the interest of a holiday in Sousse. Besides tourism, the city's main industries are wool and oil-processing.

In ancient times Sousse, with Carthage and Utica, was one of the three great Phoenician ports in Tunisia, and it retained its importance under the Romans, when it was known as Hadrumetum. The Aghlabids built the médina walls in the 9th century and set sail to conquer Sicily from here. Under the French it became the premier city of the region, and new road, rail and port facilities were built. One of the most striking features of Sousse today is that the port and the railway line are so close to the médina walls. Cargo ships unloading in the port appear to be sitting in the main street, and at night their lights blend in with those of the Place des Martyrs, the main square.

Catacombs

These ancient underground passages, which begin just outside the city centre, are said to penetrate for several miles beneath Sousse. Only a short stretch is open to the public and the chilly, claustrophobic tunnels are eerie. There is nothing really to see in the semi-darkness but they are very atmospheric. *Rue Abouel Hamad el-Ghazouli (but it's best to take a taxi because the catacombs are difficult to find). Open: Tue–Sun 8am–noon and 3–7pm. Admission charge.*

Grande Mosquée (Great Mosque)

Originally founded in the 9th century, the Great Mosque looks more like a defensive than a religious structure, and the thick, plain stone walls even have the crenellations of a fortress. The mosque never had a minaret; instead, the adjacent tower of the *ribat* was used as a vantage point from which to the call the faithful to prayer. Inside, the courtyard is pleasingly simple, with a single colonnade of horseshoe arches. All is original apart from the arcade in front of the prayer hall, which was added by the Turks in the 17th century. *Rue el-Aghlaba. Courtyard open: daily 8am–1pm, except during prayer times. Admission charge.*

View from Sousse's *ribat* tower across the médina towards the *kasbah*

The impressive tower and walls of the *Ribat*, Sousse

The Kasbah-Sousse Museum

This museum is second only to the Musée du Bardo in Tunis. Not only is it a delight to visit, but in the midday heat it is cool, with pleasant shaded gardens.

The airy rooms round the courtyard are cool and filled with beautiful mosaics displayed on the floors and the walls. The last room of the second courtyard contains the museum's finest mosaic, which can be admired from a raised viewing platform. This mosaic is exceptional for the movement that it portrays in the animals – ostriches, asses, deer and gazelle – that are about to be slaughtered by four gladiators. On the side wall is a massive statue of Priapus, the male fertility god, his head and erect penis severed by zealous Christians. From here steps lead up to the rampart walk, from where there are splendid views over the médina.

Avenue Abou Kacem ech Chabbi. Open: Tue–Sun 9am–noon, 3–6.30pm in summer; 2–5.30pm in winter. Admission charge. 57km (35 miles) northeast of Kairouan, 25km (15½ miles) west of Monastir.

The médina

Sousse's 9th-century crenellated walls were built on what was originally the shore. Except for some damage caused by Allied bombing in World War II, they are almost intact. Within the médina are three of Tunisia's most important Islamic monuments: the Great Mosque, the *Ribat* and the *Kasbah*.

Sousse

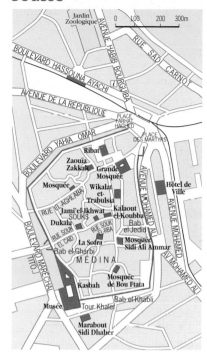

The *Ribat*

Predating the Great Mosque by some 60 years, this impressive monument is the oldest in the city. Climb the spiral-stepped tower for a spectacular view down into the courtyard of the Great Mosque, over to the port and up across the médina to the *kasbah*, built from the same golden stone. The many small rooms in the *ribat* were cells for the soldier-monks who were garrisoned here (*see p69*), while the large room at first-floor level is the prayer hall.

Rue el-Aghlaba. Open: daily 8.30am–5.30pm in winter, 8am–7pm in summer. Admission charge.

Sfax and Iles Kerkennah

Sfax is the real Tunisia. Ignore the ugly industry that surrounds the city, and explore a médina where few tourists venture. Kerkennah is pure beach-bum territory with sandy beaches, palm trees and blue sea and sky.

SFAX

Tunisia's busiest harbour and second-largest city, Sfax spreads for 20km (12½ miles) along the coast in an ugly commercial sprawl. However, the heart of the city, enclosed by 9th-century médina walls, is much more pleasant. Old Sfax is, in fact, unspoilt by tourism and is well worth a tour.

This is one of the very few Tunisian cities where you can walk through *souks* and the streets of the médina without being unduly bothered by hawkers. Making an entire inner circuit of the walls, you pass an extraordinary variety of houses, ranging from the squalid to the smart. The main route, Rue de la Grande Mosquée, skirts the wall of the Great Mosque, but as entry is restricted to Muslims, you can only peer in at the various entrances to the gloomy interior. The exterior carving is fine in many places.

Dar Jallouli Museum

The rarely visited 17th-century Arab town of Dar Jallouli has one of the most interesting museums in the country, at least on a par with the Dar Ben Abdallah in Tunis (*see pp30–31*). Erratically signposted and quite tricky to find, the Musée Régional des Arts et Traditions has rooms around a courtyard, where costumes, jewellery, beds, furniture, carved wood, calligraphy and a picture of Bouraq, Muhammad's horse, are displayed. One room is devoted to the eye make-up kohl, while another describes a fertility rite in which, on the sixth day of marriage, the couple jump to and fro over fish!

Rue de la Driba. Tel: (04) 21186. Open: Tue–Sun 9am–4.30pm. Admission charge. 125km (78 miles) south of Sousse.

ILES KERKENNAH

Moving between the beach and hotel, with a bit of windsurfing or water-skiing, is the sum total of activity for most people here. It is the beaches that make the islands special. Fine white sand runs gently into clear blue sea and palm trees line the water's edge. The islands are extremely flat, the highest point being a mere 10m (33ft), and bicycles are the favoured means of transport for those who wish to explore a little.

Most of the 15,000 inhabitants of the islands rely on the sea for their livelihood, with sponges and octopus being the main catches. The women weave palm fronds to make baskets, ropes, mats and traps for fishing. The islanders are known for their charm and good nature, as well as their good cooking.

There are two main islands – Gharbi (Arabic for 'western') and Chergui (Arabic for 'eastern'), the latter also being known as Grand Kerkennah. On Gharbi, the ferries berth at Sidi Youssef. From here, buses run along the single-track tarmacked road, through the village of Melita and across El-Kantara, a causeway originally built by the Romans, to Chergui. The beach on which most of the tourist hotels are set is Sidi Frej. A coastal path leads from the beach in front of the Grand Hotel to the ruined wall of a Roman fort, 2km (1¼ miles) away. Beyond Sidi Frej the road continues to Remla, the islands' main town, where there is a secondary school and a bank. Fishing trips can be arranged from Remla, where a fisherman will take you out on his small sailing boat, a magical experience at sunset.

20km (17½ miles) east of Sfax. This archipelago of islands, once connected to the Tunisian mainland, is reached by the SONOTRAK ferry from Sfax port. The crossing takes 1½ hours. There are six crossings a day in summer, and four from November to March.

The Kasbah in Sfax dates from the 12th century

KAIROUAN

Kairouan, Tunisia's holy city and its capital from 800 to 1057, has the country's finest concentration of Islamic buildings. Invariably dusty, hot, dirty and full of tenacious carpet-dealers, it is not an easy place to visit, yet, despite this, it is worth the hassle. For the faint-hearted, an organised tour is the best way to see the city.

Kairouan, meaning 'caravan', was so named by the Arab leader Aqba Ben Nafi, who led his troops into Tunisia from Egypt, setting up his base here in 670. He chose this site because there were already deep wells here and grazing for his horses. This was also a strategic position from which to control the steppe land and attack the fortified Byzantine cities of the coast. Lying inland from the more cosmopolitan coast, Kairouan has remained a purely Arab, Islamic city. Christians and Jews were not permitted to enter it until the French occupation of 1881.

Bassins des Aghlabides (Aghlabid Pools)

Ibrahim Ibn Aghlab founded his dynasty in AD 800, with Kairouan as the capital. The following century was the golden age of Kairouan, which derived its wealth from the trans-Saharan caravan trade. These impressive pools, the largest of several cisterns and pools around Kairouan, were built in the 9th century to collect winter rainwater and flashflood water for use in the dry months of summer. Tucked away from the bustle of the city centre, a stroll around this 9th-century feat of engineering is a pleasure.
Avenue de la République.
Open: daily 8am–5pm.
Admission charge covered by joint ticket for all sites.

SEEING THE SIGHTS

The main sights are scattered about the city so it makes sense to go on an organised tour. This will usually include a stroll round the *souk*.

Unrestored Aghlabid pool outside Kairouan

Kairouan

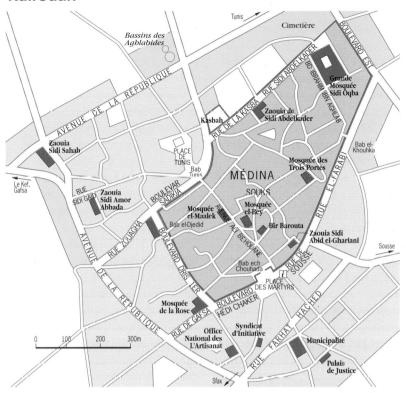

Map labels: Tunis, Bassins des Aghlabides, Cimetière, BOULEVARD EST, RUE SIDI ABDELKADER, BD IBRAHIM IBN AGHLAB, Grande Mosquée Sidi Oqba, AVENUE DE LA REPUBLIQUE, Kasbah, RUE DE LA KASBAH, Zaouia de Sidi Abdelkader, Bab el-Khouhka, Zaouia Sidi Sahab, PLACE DE TUNIS, Bab Tunis, MÉDINA, Mosquée des Trois Portes, Le Kef, Gafsa, RUE SIDI GAID, Zaouia Sidi Amor Abbada, BOULEVARD SADIKIA, RUE ZOUAGHA, SOUKS, Mosquée el-Maalek, Bab el-Djedid, AVENUE ALI BEHOUANE, Mosquée el-Bey, RUE EL-FARABI, Bir Barouta, Zaouia Sidi Abid el-Ghariani, Sousse, AVENUE DE LA REPUBLIQUE, BOULEVARD DRISS I'ER, Bab ech Chouhada, RUE DE SOUSSE, PLACE DES MARTYRS, Mosquée de la Rose, BOULEVARD HEDI CHAKER, RUE DE GAFSA, Office National des L'Artisanat, Syndicat d'Initiative, RUE FARHAT HACHED, Municipalité, Palais de Justice, Sfax

0   100   200   300m

Grande Mosquée Sidi Oqba

Built originally in AD 670, this is the oldest place of Muslim worship in North Africa and the holiest building in Tunisia. When the rest of the city was destroyed in a Bedouin assault, it was the only building to be spared. The original mosque has long since disappeared, as have the four mosques later built on the same site. The present mosque was built by the Aghlabites in 863. It is striking for its sheer size and simplicity, and entering the vast paved courtyard you are struck by the silence and overwhelmed by a sense of awe. Within the courtyard are seven well-heads, now covered by column bases that sit over the cisterns. Buckets of water were once drawn from these wells for ritual ablution before prayer. Look closely at the columns and capitals surrounding the courtyard to spot Roman relics of Carthage and Sousse.

Although only Muslims may enter the prayer hall, its hefty carved wooden doorways allow non-Muslims a glimpse of the dark interior, with its forest of pillars. The 9th-century *minbar* (pulpit), tantalisingly out of sight, is said to be the oldest in the world. The tall, solid minaret once had a defensive role. Today it is occasionally left open and non-Muslims are allowed to climb the 128 steps to the top for fine views over the city and the mosque.

Boulevard Ibrahim Ibn Aghlab. Open: Sat–Thur 8am–12.30pm, 4.30–6.30pm in summer, 3–4.30pm in winter. Also Fri 8am–noon. Admission charge – joint ticket to all sites. Photography permitted in the courtyard.

The médina

The present walls of the médina date from the 11th century. The usual entry point is through Bab ech Chouhada (Martyrs' Gate). Up the first alleyway to the right after 100m (110yds) is the Zaouia Sidi Abid el-Ghariani, a 14th-century Sufi shrine, restored in the 17th century. As the building has now been

The minaret of the Grande Mosquée Sidi Oqba

desanctified, the saint's body having been removed elsewhere, it is open to non-Muslims. Note the elaborate decoration on the doors, floors and courtyard walls.

The Mosquée des Trois Portes (Mosque of the Three Doors) is rarely visited by tourists because it involves a slightly complicated route. Its extraordinary 9th-century façade has three doors carved from stone. Built by an Andalucian, it is one of the few early remnants of the old city. Non-Muslims are not permitted to enter.

Continue back on the main route through the médina (Avenue Ali Behouane, formerly Avenue Habib Bourguiba), and you know you have reached the centre of the médina when you arrive at the cluster of buildings that form an island in the middle of the street. These are the Café el-Halfaouine, the Mosquée el-Bey (Mosque of the Bey) and the famous Bir Barouta (Well of Barouta), recognisable by its green-tiled roof. The name comes from a Kairouan legend, Barouta being the name of Oqba Ibn Nafi's dog, which is said to have dug up the ground to find this spring. Climb to the first floor of the Bir Barouta to sample the holy water, which is drawn from the well by a blindfolded camel that circles incessantly to pump the water. Drinking it is said to guarantee that you will return to Kairouan. Beyond this island, three arches lead through to the main covered *souk*, which is not large

SIGHTS

An all-inclusive ticket gives you entrance to the major sights. The ticket office is beside the Aghlabid Pools (*see p78*), opposite the Hotel Continental, open: 8am–5pm. All the sights, except for the pools, the Zaouia of Sidi Sahab and Zaouia Sidi Amor Abbada, are inside the médina.

but which hums with activity. The main road ends at the impressive Bab Tunis (Tunis Gate), which is surmounted by a guardhouse. Note its ancient columns and the colossal iron-studded gates. Zaouia Sidi Abid el-Ghariani and Bir Barouta are covered by the joint ticket.

Zaouia Sidi Amor Abbada

This 19th-century shrine is rarely visited because it lies well outside the médina and is quite tricky to find. It has five domes and much of the interior is filled with wooden or wrought-iron furniture. The holy man to whom the *zaouia* is dedicated was an illiterate blacksmith who made doom-laden predictions such as this one: 'Three great serpents, covered with scales and vomiting iron and fire, will encircle Kairouan with their tracks and finding no defenders will penetrate into the city as a punishment for the numerous crimes committed there for centuries past.' Local opinion has it that this prophecy was fulfilled when Allied tanks entered the médina in 1943. *Rue Sidi Gaid. Open: daily 8am–5pm. Admission charge covered by the joint ticket.*

Zaouia Sidi Sahab (Shrine of the Barber)

One of the most beautiful of all religious buildings in Kairouan, this *zaouia* is a delight to visit because it is still imbued with a feeling of current pilgrimage and is popular with families and children. In this place of joy and laughter, newborn babies are blessed and even circumcised, and in hot weather it is pleasurable to linger in the shade watching these family scenes. The complex is large and spacious, with an outer brick courtyard from which an elaborate tiled corridor leads through to a marble hall, Beyond is the sanctuary courtyard, with the saint's tomb. Sidi Sahab, one of the companions of the Prophet Muhammad, was known as the Barber because he used to wear a locket round his neck containing hairs from the Prophet's beard.
Avenue de la République. Open: daily 8.30am–5.30pm. Admission charge covered by the joint ticket.

Exterior of the Zaouia of Sidi Sahab, Kairouan's most accessible monument

Islamic architecture

Wander around the médina of any old town in North Africa and exotic-looking buildings – with smooth, white, rounded domes, slender pointed minarets or perfectly formed horseshoe arches – will have you reaching for your camera. However, the fundamental difference between Islamic and Western architecture does not lie in the shapes of buildings. Look beyond them and you will notice that the architect's objective is nearly always to create an indoor, inward-looking space with all its rooms and windows looking on to a private internal courtyard. By contrast, Western architecture concentrates on the location of buildings and the positions of their windows, so as to maximise their views to the outside. While climate is obviously a major factor, the Islamic building style also reflects a difference in philosophy. In Islam the home is a private and

Traditional horseshoe arches

inward-looking place where women can walk about freely, unseen by strangers and passers-by, and into which outsiders are rarely invited. Larger houses have a bench-lined hall corridor (*driba*), which connects with the courtyard. However, the corridor is bent in a dog-leg shape so that the courtyard is not visible, and here male visitors would be entertained, away from the women of the house.

In Tunisia the earliest Islamic buildings are the *ribats* (fortified monasteries) at Monastir and Sousse. The distinguishing feature of these early buildings (also seen in the great mosques) is the horseshoe arch, which often rests on pillars salvaged from classical sites. The domes of mosques and *zaouias* (tomb complexes) were drawn from Byzantine architecture. The influence of Moorish Spain began under the Almohad and Hafsid dynasties of the 12th to 14th centuries and continues even today in Tunisian tilework. Few public buildings in the Andalucian style now remain, although the town of Sidi Bou Said shows its strong influence.

Mosques tend to comprise a simple open-plan courtyard, enclosed by a high, outer, windowless wall; within is the ablution fountain for the ritual washing of hands and feet before prayer. At the end of the courtyard is the carpeted prayer hall, where shoes

Decorative calligraphy

are removed. The main decorative feature inside the hall is the *mihrab* (prayer niche), which indicates the direction of Mecca, which the congregation must face during prayer. In larger mosques there is a *minbar* (pulpit), reached by a steep flight of steps, from which the prayer leader delivers the special Friday morning prayer. Any internal decoration is usually concentrated on the *mihrab* and the *minbar*, otherwise mosque interiors are uncluttered and simple.

The *minaret* (mosque tower) is the vantage point from which the *muezzin* (prayer leader) summons the faithful to prayer, with a haunting ritualised call that rings out from all mosques five times a day.

Drive: Kairouan to Makthar

This drive takes you through some extraordinary gorge-like scenery in the interior of Tunisia, together with some unusual forest, to reach one of the Tell's most impressive Roman cities at Makthar, then returns via the well-preserved fortress of Ksar Lemsa. Most of the drive is on near-deserted roads and there is little habitation, so go well provided with food and drink.

Allow half a day.

1 Kairouan

Leaving Kairouan on route 99, you follow empty roads, which lead through deserted landscapes, a welcome contrast to the bustle of the city.

2 Ousseltia

Ousseltia is the first sizeable town that you come to. Notice the colonial church, a relic of the French who founded the town in 1927 as a centre for the surrounding groves of olives and almond trees.

3 Ksar Lemsa

For an optional detour, fork north off the main road just before Ousseltia to reach Ksar Lemsa. This impressively

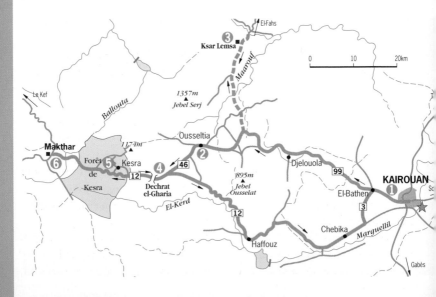

Returning home to the little hillside village of Kesra

5 Kesra

This Berber village is built into the hillside, though it is less impressive than the fortified hilltop Berber villages of the south, such as Chenini. Around the edge of the village there are several *koubbas* (domes), the tombs of local holy men.

The road between Kesra and Makthar passes through some of Tunisia's most beautiful scenery, with gorges and valleys with trees, flowers and pastureland.

You can turn off a sidetrack into the forest to enjoy a peaceful picnic away from habitation. Drive up from a valley onto a high plateau and you will reach Makthar.

well-preserved 6th-century Byzantine fortress stands at the foot of an escarpment. Its towers and battlements are still intact, and inside the courtyard architectural fragments are arranged in the custodian's garden.

Head back to route 99 and on past Ousseltia until you reach route 46, then continue until you hit the main road, route 12, when you turn in the direction of Makthar.

4 Dechrat el-Gharia

This extraordinary rock formation, consisting of dramatic needle-shaped rocks, can be seen where the road passes through a tunnel.

A few kilometres further on, you reach the Forêt de Kesra (Forest of Kesra), a carpet of green Aleppo pines. Take the detour here up to the village of Kesra.

6 Makthar

Makthar is a curious place, divided into old and new by a Roman triumphant arch that marks the spot where there was once a spring. Directly opposite the arch is Makthar's interesting museum, which also gives access to the Roman site. Makthar's most impressive monuments lie well away from this entrance, so you may initially be disappointed. However, if you persevere, you will be rewarded by the discovery of some truly spectacular Roman buildings.

Museum. Open: 9am–noon, 2–6pm in summer, 2–5.30pm in winter.

From Makthar you can return directly to Kairouan via Haffouz on route 12 in just over an hour.

The interior

The principal town of the Tell region is Le Kef, which is a good base and which, with Roman and Byzantine remains, is of considerable interest in its own right. To the southwest, near the Algerian border, are some dramatic mountain formations. The most unusual, the Table de Jugurtha, is of particular interest to walkers.

Continuing southwards, the Tell becomes increasingly arid, offering no more than rough grazing. Gafsa was as far south as the Romans ventured. Still further south, around the vast salt lake of Chott el-Jerid, the desert begins. Chott el-Jerid is the largest of several salt lakes. It is fringed with some beautiful, lush oases that contrast with the scorching white salt flats. Tozeur and Nefta are the most famous of these oases. Both are worth a visit in their own right and they are also good bases for forays into the Sahara.

Around Tamerza, a little way to the north of Chott el-Jerid, is perhaps the most dramatic scenery in Tunisia. Here a collection of small oases are set in sandy gorges cut into the side of great sandstone mountains watered by springs and waterfalls.

Aridness and fertility juxtaposed at the mountain oasis of Tamerza

For a taste of the desert, without the hardship of a trek into the Sahara itself, visit Douz. This small oasis village gives tourists the chance to ride a camel through Sahara-like landscapes within easy reach of their hotel, before returning to the luxury of shade and a drink by the pool.

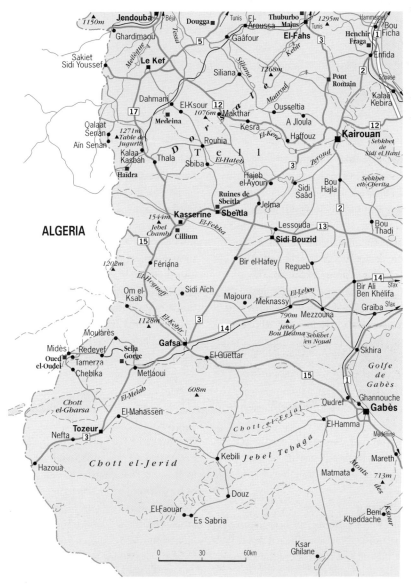

Dougga

Dougga is Tunisia's showpiece Roman site and features prominently in tourist brochures and on posters. A full tour could take several hours, but certainly a minimum of 1½ hours should be allowed for the visit.

Background

Founded in the 4th century BC, Dougga is one of the oldest towns of the Tunisian interior. It is one of the most complete Roman cities, with more temples than any other in North Africa. Despite its size, however, its population never exceeded 5,000. A relic of its early Carthaginian origins is the remarkable tall, pointed mausoleum at the lowest level of the site. Most of the extant Roman buildings date from the 2nd century AD. With the spread of Christianity, Dougga and its pagan temples were gradually eclipsed, so that, when the Byzantines conquered Tunisia in the 6th century, Dougga was nothing more than a farming village, its ancient stones pillaged for building elsewhere.

Site tour

The Roman theatre, the best-preserved in Tunisia, is cut into the natural slope of the hill and the first building you see when you enter the site. The stage building is unusually complete, and the tiers of seating could accommodate 3,500 people. The theatre is still used for the performance of classical plays every August.

Climb out over the top steps of the theatre and follow the little path up the hillside towards the tall columns of the Temple of Saturn. From here, there are fine views over the valley, but beware unfenced holes as you gaze at the scenery. Look out for the footprints in the temple's stone floor, said to be those either of the god Saturn himself or of a Roman emperor.

Retrace your steps back to the theatre and follow the path towards the unmistakable Capitol Temple, the most perfectly preserved building of its kind in Tunisia. The beautiful golden stone of its Corinthian portico glows ethereally at sunset. On the way, you cross the circular Plaza of the Winds, named for the 12 Roman winds carved in its paving stones, then pass the Temple of Mercury.

Following the paved street beyond the Capitol Temple downhill for some 100m (110yds), you come to the colonnaded courtyard of the Temple of Liber Pater on your right. Directly opposite are the high walls of the impressive Baths of Licinius, reached by two flights of stairs or through a service tunnel into what was once the baths' vast main hall.

Another 50m (55yds) or so further downhill, a fork leads to the small Cyclops Bath. Its communal latrines are arranged in horseshoe formation, with keyhole-shapes cut into the stones, for a dozen occupants to sit and chat together. Beside the baths is the Trifolium Brothel, where a staircase leads down into a sunken courtyard. Off the courtyard are small booths where the prostitutes sat, waiting for their clients.

Continue downhill to the distinctive pyramid-topped tower, the Libyco-Punic Mausoleum of Ateban. This unique relic of the Punic era, built around 200 BC, combines Egyptian, Greek and Persian architectural features, and merits close inspection. Of particular interest are the Persian-style animal carvings depicting the soul's journey in chariots drawn through the heavens by four horses. *117km (73 miles) southwest of Tunis. Site open: daily dawn–dusk. Admission charge.*

Sunset views from the theatre at Dougga make the climb worthwhile

Roman Africa

For some two to three centuries from 30 BC onwards, this part of North Africa was the most politically stable province of the Roman Empire, and was of tremendous importance to Rome, producing two-thirds of its grain needs (Egypt provided the other third). Under the Roman Empire, African citizens were free to work their way up to senior administrative positions. Many became Roman senators and indeed Septimus Severus was the first Roman emperor of African origin. Roman Africa was also remarkable for the number of its towns and cities, in which prominent local people would display their wealth by having public buildings erected in their honour. These towns were built to a set pattern, with the forum at the centre, a rectangular paved courtyard surrounded by shops and the town's main administrative and religious buildings. The major religious building, always set on the forum, was called the Capitol. This was a temple dedicated to the three patron gods of the empire, Jupiter (city and state), his wife Juno (protector of the Roman people) and Minerva (protector of commerce and industry). All major towns had at least one set of baths, huge structures with vaulted ceilings, which were frequented not only for personal cleanliness but which also functioned as centres for socialising. They also included libraries with reading rooms. Towns in Roman Africa were linked by the excellent roads and bridges that were built to facilitate trade.

Roman Africa's greatest artistic legacy is its mosaics, which are found in profusion both in public buildings and private houses, and which are of a higher standard of workmanship than that of mosaics elsewhere in the Roman Empire.

Bulla Regia mosaics in northern Tunisia

Hannibal, scourge of Rome
Hannibal, the famous Carthaginian general who succeeded his father Hamilcar Barca in 221 BC, at the age of 25, was Rome's fiercest opponent during the Punic Wars. Hannibal

launched his major attack on Rome in 218 BC. Having marched through Spain and France, then crossed the Alps with 300 elephants and 40,000 men, Hannibal won many battles as he moved south towards Rome. Just as the city seemed to be at his mercy, support from Carthage was cut off and he was eventually ordered to return. Back in Tunisia he was finally defeated by the Roman general Scipio at the Battle of Zama (near Le Kef) in 202 BC. Hannibal's fiery legend lived on for many years, and Roman mothers would silence their children with the warning 'Hannibal is coming'.

Haïdra lies near the frontier with Algeria

EXPLORING THE INTERIOR
Haïdra

The most remote of all Tunisia's Roman sites, Haïdra (Ammaedra in ancient times) lies a few kilometres from the border with Algeria. Continuously inhabited since the 1st century BC, Haïdra was founded by the Carthaginians, taken over by the Romans and then finally by the Byzantines because there were springs in the nearby river valley and because this was a strategic location for defending the border.

The remains of five churches here are evidence of an active Early Christian community. A settlement survived here till 1939, and the most recent ruin is the French frontier fort built in 1886 to the right of the road as you approach from Kalaa.

Kasbah

The modern road cuts straight through the forum of the ancient town, with the ruins lying scattered mainly to the south of the road. The site has never been systematically excavated. Many of the Roman monuments are still partially buried, leaving the Byzantine buildings as the most immediately visible. The best-preserved of Haïdra's Roman monuments is the large arch of Septimus Severus, from which a stretch of Roman paving leads into the town. Also dramatic is the Orange or Porticoed Mausoleum, a tall conical structure standing alone in the scrubland due south of the archway.

A colossal Byzantine fort, the Kasbah, one of the largest in North Africa, dominates the site. For the best view of this, follow the tarmacked road that forks left to run alongside the riverbed. A Roman bridge once spanned the gorge, giving access to the fort, but it collapsed, so you have to wade through the shallow waters. You must enter the fort to fully appreciate its scale, and climb the stairways to reach the battlements.

78km (48 miles) northwest of Kasserine, 79km (49 miles) south of Le Kef. Always open. Free.

Table de Jugurtha

Rising above the foothills near the border with Algeria, this gigantic table mountain is an unforgettable sight (*see pp94–5*). From a distance it seems totally inaccessible, but as you approach, you will see a tarmacked road, which ascends to within 4km (2½ miles) of the summit. The plateau is named after Jugurtha, king of Numidia in the 2nd century BC, who retreated here with his garrison. On the summit, which commands a remarkable view, cows graze among the remains of fortifications.

72km (45 miles) southwest of Le Kef.

Kasserine

A dull, unattractive town that stretches out on either side of the road, Kasserine has little to recommend it apart from being a base at which to stock up on food, petrol and other provisions.

Kasserine means 'two forts', a reference to the two Roman mausoleums that survive here. On the Gafsa road out of town, beside the circular Hotel Cillium, lie the scant remains of the Roman town of Cillium, dating back to the 1st century BC. Today it makes a pleasant picnic spot. Immediately to the west of the town is Jebel Chambi, Tunisia's highest mountain. Rising to 1,544m (5,066ft), it is popular with hill-walkers and boar-hunters.

158km (98 miles) southwest of Kairouan, 120km (75 miles) south of Le Kef.

Roman temple at Kasserine

Walk: Table de Jugurtha

An exhilarating experience in a unique mountain landscape, the walk up Jugurtha's Table Mountain involves a steep ascent up rock-cut steps. There is a hotel restaurant at Qalaat Senan, a village near the mountain, where you can enjoy energy-restoring food and drink. The walk is not suitable for the elderly or the very young.

Allow about 3 hours.

From afar, as you head towards the Algerian border, the mountain is immediately recognisable by its flat summit. It looks dauntingly unassailable, with apparently sheer sides all round.

Qalaat Senan (85km/53 miles north of Kasserine) is the nearest village, a modern settlement in the valley below the mountain. Towards the end of the town, a blue sign points left to Aïn

Senan. Follow the tarmacked road as it winds up to the hamlet that sits at the very foot of the mountain.

At the hamlet, fork left up another tarmacked road that passes an extremely smart house on its own promontory. The road peters out into a stony track accessible only to four-wheel-drive vehicles.

The 4km (2½-mile) walk up this track takes around 1 hour 15 minutes,

The distinctive table shape of the mountain

Towards the Algerian border from the plateau of Jugurtha's Table Mountain

hugging the left side of the table mountain, whose sheer cliffs loom impressively above. Jugurtha, king of Numidia, was noted for his aggression, and he chose this natural fortress to garrison his army from 112 to 105 BC, while he confronted the invading Romans. In Byzantine times the summit was again used as a stronghold, this time by a local bandit called Senan and his men, who held out here from the tax-collecting troops of the ruling *beys*. The modern local name for the mountain is Qalaat Senan (like the village). The views from this stretch of the track are breathtakingly beautiful and very dramatic.

The last section of the ascent is steeper, and the stones underfoot are loose and slippery. The path ends at the rock-cut stairway, and from here the climb up takes no more than 15 minutes. The steps are uneven and a bit of scrambling is often required. Near the top is the Byzantine gateway built by the bandit Senan.

At the summit you are almost in another world. Cows graze among the ruins of the many houses where the various troops were garrisoned, and troglodytic caves and extensive cisterns dating from Byzantine times can be found. The path from the top of the stairway leads directly to the marabout, the little whitewashed dome where the body of Sidi Abd el-Jouad, a local saint, is buried. Unusually, visitors are permitted, and even encouraged, to enter the shrine to see the simple draped tomb inside, where candles usually burn in memory of the saint. The local people seem to enjoy climbing the fortress too, and especially at weekends they make excursions to visit the shrine and request special favours of the saint.

Le Kef

Vibrant Le Kef is the most significant town of inland Tunisia after Kairouan. It has always been politically active. During World War II it was the seat of a government opposed to Vichy France, and later it became the headquarters of the Free French. Habib Bourguiba's second wife was born in Le Kef, and the president built a fine palace here, which unfortunately is now crumbling and unused.

Kef means 'rock' in Arabic, a reference to the town's dramatic setting on a high escarpment overlooking rolling hills. Le Kef's main sights today are the double *kasbah* on the hilltop, a few Roman buildings dating from the 2nd–3rd century AD, when the town, known as Sicca Veneria, was a centre for the worship of Venus, and Byzantine buildings dating from the 5th century onwards, when the town was an important monastic centre.

Cannons guarding the entrance to the *kasbah* at Le Kef

Dar el-Kouss Church

This is also known as St Peter's Church. It is quite large and well preserved, although it has no roof.

Kasbah

At the highest point of the town, approached from the wide boulevard off Avenue Habib Bourguiba that leads up past the presidential palace, sits the impressive double *kasbah*. This 17th–18th-century Turkish fort was built on earlier Byzantine foundations. From the *kasbah* there are some fantastic views of the town and the surrounding countryside.

Place Bou Makhlouf

This charming square near the *kasbah* has a few cafés and is an excellent place to sit and admire the town's setting, with views down over the plain.

On one side of the square is the plain stone building known as the Jemaa el-Kebir (Old Mosque), which now serves as the regional museum of antiquities. At the end of the square is the tiny mosque of Sidi Bou Makhlouf, with two domes and an ornate minaret.

Tourbet d'Ali Turki

Up the hill from the Palais Presidential, on the way to the *kasbah*, is the derelict Tourbet (mausoleum) of Ali Turki, father of the founder of the Husseinite dynasty (1704–1881). In Ottoman times, Le Kef was deeply embroiled in the struggle for power. Hussein bin Ali, a Turkish soldier of Greek origin and the founder of the Husseinite dynasty, had his headquarters here.

Sidi Bou Makhlouf Mosque: one of the mosques on Place Bou Makhlouf

Walk: Le Kef *kasbah*

Le Kef, the main town of Tunisia's mountainous hinterland, is dominated by its mighty kasbah. *This walk leads from the centre of town, along the tortuous alleys of the old town and up to the* kasbah *and the cluster of interesting buildings immediately below it. You can break your walk at the café in the pleasant open square near the top.*

Allow about 2 hours, the first half-hour of which you will spend climbing to the summit, with the remainder for exploring the buildings, and then the descent. Begin at the site of the old Roman spring (Aïn el-Kef).

1 Aïn el-Kef

The Roman spring gushes from a hollow opposite the Hôtel Sicca Veneria on Place de l'Indépendance. Roman stonework with an accompanying nymph can still be seen around the spring. The nymph has become the focus of an Islamic sect, and offerings are often placed here. In summer there is an open-air café. *Above it is the Hôtel de la Source.*

2 Hôtel de la Source

This hotel is famous for its most luxurious bedroom, a splendid example of 19th-century Tunisian domestic architecture decorated with stucco and tilework. Nearby is the entrance to a huge cistern (now kept locked), which used to supply the Roman public baths. *Follow the steep alleyway to the right of the Hôtel de la Source, for a taste of street life in the old town. As you near the top, the great wall of the* kasbah *looms up and you follow it to the entrance gateway.*

3 & 4 *Kasbah* forts

There are two forts here, an upper and a lower. The first entrance, lined with a row of Turkish cannons, is into the lower fort (3), the older and larger fort of the two. Built in 1601, it was used as a prison for Tunisian nationalists in the 20th century. A path leads round to the impressive hill gateway into the upper fort (4). Built by the Ottoman *bey* in 1740, it is approached over a drawbridge and was used as barracks

A typical steep, narrow street in Le Kef

by the French. It stands on the site of an older fort, and has probably been remodelled many times over the years. From the battlements there are views westwards across the plain and over to the mountains near the Algerian border. *Leave the* kasbah *again and enter Place Bou Makhlouf.*

5 Jemaa el-Kebir

This plain stone building, known today as the Old Mosque, is something of a mystery. It was originally built in the 4th century, but its exact purpose remains obscure. Theories as to its function range from its serving from almost everything from a marketplace to a temple of prostitution. Since the Arab conquest, it has been used as a mosque, although its minaret has been removed. Inside is a fine colonnaded courtyard from which a gate leads to a cross-shaped room with a barrel-vaulted ceiling. Above the Old Mosque are stairs leading up to the Mosquée de Sidi Bou Makhlouf.

6 Mosquée de Sidi Bou Makhlouf

With its domes and minaret, this mosque is quite distinctive. Further on is the Café des Andalous, where you can rest before the descent.

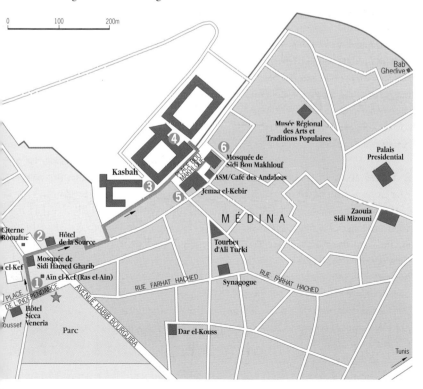

Makthar

Makthar was founded in the 2nd century BC. However, the major monuments that remain today are Roman and date mainly from the 2nd century AD. Abandoned in the 11th century, the town was forgotten until it was rediscovered in the 19th century by the French colonists who established modern Makthar.

The surrounding scenery is dramatic, but the entrance to Makthar itself is spectacular. Climb up the pathway and then head towards the monumental Arch of Trajan. From here, the true grandeur of the site unfolds. A paved street leads past a fine basilica to your left, then drops down to the splendid Roman baths whose walls still tower high. Although the baths were converted into a fortress by the Byzantines, the floors are still covered in abstract and wave-pattern mosaics, and it is easy to imagine the leisurely lifestyle once enjoyed here.

Turn back towards the Arch of Trajan and take the other main paved street past the huge forum to the left and the Temple of Bacchus to the right, forking left at the next crossroads and heading for the tree-covered building on the right of the street. Known as the Schola, this was the clubhouse for élite young men of the town who formed a sort of constabulary. Beyond the clubhouse is a jumble of graves and megalithic tombs. Further on, outside the boundary stands a tall, neo-Punic mausoleum with a pyramidal roof.

69km (43 miles) southeast of Le Kef, 114km (71 miles) northwest of Kairouan. Open: daily 8am–7pm in summer, 8.30am–5.30pm in winter. Admission charge.

Medeina

Little visited because of its remoteness, Medeina is not an isolated site, however, for it lies in a natural bowl ringed by rural hamlets. This has its charm in that village life, with flocks of sheep, braying donkeys and incessant water-collecting, goes on around you, lending the ruins an incongruous air of lived-in normality.

Founded by the Carthaginians in the 2nd century BC, Medeina (ancient Althiburos) was an outpost on the military road between Carthage and Tebessa (in what is now Algeria). The town reached its peak under the Emperor Hadrian (AD 117–138), and most of the extant buildings date from this period. It continued for a while as a Byzantine outpost, but declined after the Arab conquest, although the village of Medeina survives because of its perennial springs.

A large triumphal arch marks the entrance to the site, and from the paved street you can climb the steps to the left to enter the vast paved forum. Scattered about are Corinthian capitals carved from rich golden stone, and the base for a statue complete with inscription and foot-holes. Higher up, the crumbling ruins of the Capitol temple can no longer be approached as the

The Schola of Juvenes is one of the Roman buildings in Makthar

steps have collapsed. Follow the Roman street towards the remains of the theatre arches, passing a monumental fountain. Below the forum you will notice two buildings on the other side of the riverbed, both palatial private houses whose mosaics are now in the Musée du Bardo in Tunis. One, called the Building of Aesculapius, was converted into impressive public baths in the 4th century, with mosaic-lined bathhouses, pools and fountains.

38km (23¹/₂ miles) south of Le Kef. Open: daily from dawn to sunset. Admission charge.

Sbeïtla

Sbeïtla, known as Sufetula in Roman times, is the most southerly of Tunisia's major Roman sites. It is the country's second most impressive Roman city after Dougga. At its peak, the city's inhabitants numbered 10,000, double that of modern Sbeïtla. For a brief time

Remains of Medeina's Roman theatre

The impressive Roman remains at Sbeïtla are built from fine golden stone

in the 7th century, Sbeïtla was the capital of a rogue emperor, the Patriarch Gregory, who decided to rebel against Byzantine control from Constantinople. His glory was short-lived, however, for the following year Arab armies overran the town, killing Gregory and stealing his riches.

The sheer scale of the Roman public buildings here is impressive. The entrance to the site, the museum and the ticket booth are on the main road from Kasserine. The museum has a few good mosaics and statues that were discovered at the site, notably a depiction of Bacchus, god of wine, sprawled in a drunken stupor.

The site entrance is well tended and pretty flowers line the path down to the splendid triumphal arch to the right. The path then leads to the left past a pair of 6th-century Byzantine forts, well preserved and sturdily constructed in the rich golden stone that was used for all such buildings. Beyond the forts the path leads into a main paved street. Turn right at the crossroads to explore the extensive baths, with their plunge pools and now-fragmentary mosaics, then on downhill to the ruined theatre, unusually situated at the lowest level of the town, overlooking the river gorge. It was here that the statue of Bacchus in the museum was found.

Thuburbo Majus, with the Temple of Mercury in the background

Walk back up the main paved street towards the trio of the Capitol temples, passing the Church of Severus, with its many broken columns, on your right. The entrance to the impressive forum is marked by an ancient gateway, and the walls that now enclose the forum area are not Roman but Byzantine defences for protection against Berber attacks. The Roman forum and three temples, dating from the 2nd century AD, are one of Tunisia's most magnificent sights. In other towns, such as Dougga, the Capitoline trio were worshipped in one temple, but here the three deities – Jupiter, Juno and Minerva – were each accorded individual shrines. The largest, central temple was devoted to Jupiter, king of the gods. It has elaborately carved capitals and tooth-shaped stones illustrating ancient roof-construction techniques. The chambers below are especially well preserved.

Leaving via the tunnel that leads out behind the temples, head towards the basilica and church on the right. The 6th-century basilica of Vitalis contains two interesting features: a fish mosaic in the central basin, and a walk-in baptismal font, in excellent condition and covered in mosaics. The strange shape of the font, reminiscent of a blancmange, has been likened to a vulva, symbolic of second birth through baptism. Beyond these churches lie nothing more of interest except the scant remains of an amphitheatre. *Museum. Open: daily dawn to sunset. Admission charge. 40km (25 miles)* *northeast of Kasserine, 164km (102 miles) southwest of Sousse.*

Thuburbo Majus

One of Tunisia's most impressive sites, Thuburbo Majus has a fine setting, overlooking the valley and backed by hills. Its major buildings date from the 2nd century AD, although many were restored and extended in the 4th century. The entrance path leads straight to the colossal fluted columns of the Capitol temple, where Jupiter, Juno and Minerva, the three chief deities of the Roman state, were worshipped. Immediately behind is the forum and to the right the Temple of Mercury is recognisable by its circle of columns in the courtyard. Beyond the forum, a little to the right, are the Summer Baths, marked by an elegant line of grey marble and columns which flank the exercise courtyard known as the Palaestra of the Petronii, after the wealthy family who endowed it in AD 225.

Further up the hill are the Winter Baths. Forming an impressive complex to the left of the path, they are remarkably well preserved inside, with attractive black and white diamond mosaic flooring and brown-veined marble columns. There are no refreshment facilities on the site, but picnicking is permitted and the Winter Baths make an excellent shady spot. *63km (39 miles) south of Tunis, 91km (57 miles) north of Kairouan. Open: daily 8am–5pm. Admission charge.*

The Chotts and oasis towns

The salt flats (chotts) on the fringes of the Sahara are mirage inducing. The magic of the oasis towns provides cooling respite from the arid desert and the best dates in the world, too.

Chebika

This is the southernmost of a cluster of three notable oases close by the Algerian border (the other two being Tamerza and Midès). Chebika, at the very edge of the mountains, looks out over the bleak expanse of a salt lake, Chott el-Gharsa. From here a road leads across the salt flats to Tozeur. However, between October and April, flooding frequently makes this route impassable. Behind the village, a narrow gorge with palm trees and cascades makes for a pleasant stroll. *60km (37 miles) north of Tozeur, 5km (3 miles) south of Tamerza.*

A basic refreshment stop halfway across the Chott causeway

Chott el-Jerid

Covering some 5,000sq km (1,900sq miles), Chott el-Jerid is the largest salt lake in North Africa, one of several that spread from here westwards into Algeria. The extent of the lakes shown on most maps is the maximum that they cover during the winter months, when rainfall is heaviest. In the summer the lakes turn into a white salty expanse, which shimmers with mirages but which is devoid of life as no plant or fish can survive in such conditions. However, around the edge of the *chott* (meaning 'salt flat' in Arabic) springs feed oases where date palms grow. From these oases nomads move out across the pebbly scrubland with their herds of camels and goats, drifting ever onwards to find fresh grazing land.

Today, Chott el-Jerid can easily be crossed via the causeway built by the army. Along the way there are stopping places from which you can view the red mineral deposits that colour the lake in places and perhaps even see a mirage (most likely in the hottest part of the day). In the days before wheeled transport, the camel route across the *chott* was marked by lines of palm-tree trunks. At the midpoint was a raised circular platform where the camel caravans could spend the night safely. *88km (55 miles) south of Gafsa, 122km (76 miles) west of Gabès.*

Douz

This tiny place has built up a name for itself as the tourist centre for forays

Chebika oasis

into the Sahara either by four-wheel-drive vehicle or by camel. Arriving here from Chott el-Jerid, you feel as if you are heading towards the edge of the world and into the vast emptiness of the desert. Despite the tourist activity here, Douz is still a quiet place, and only really comes to life with its Thursday market, which inevitably features some camel trading. The town is also the centre for the 15,000-strong nomadic Mrazig tribe, who raise sheep and goats.

If you decide to take one trip from your beach resort out to the Sahara, you should choose go to somewhere like Douz, which is on the edge of the Grand Erg Oriental (Great Sandy Dune Desert). At the road past the tourist hotels you climb over the first set of dunes; from there sand dunes stretch

Douz market

steps leading down into the bubbling hot water, whose average temperature is 31°C (88°F). From the pools you can see the octagonal minaret of Gafsa's Great Mosque, which is closed to non-Muslims. A small museum beside the pools displays mosaics from Zammour, a minor site near Medenine. Enjoy a coffee at the pleasant Café des Piscines Romaines before moving on. Back along Avenue Habib Bourguiba the heavily restored *kasbah* is also closed to visitors, and immediately behind it you can see the edge of the oasis. Gafsa is famous for its pistachio nuts. Other local specialities are baskets and mats woven from palm fronds.

Museum. Open: Tue–Sun 8am–noon, 2–6pm. Admission charge.
93km (58 miles) northeast of Tozeur.

out before you as far as the eye can see. This is the soft, sandy desert of our imagination and not the inhospitable, rocky ground that is in fact the more common desert terrain.
30km (18¹/₂ miles) south of Kebili.

Gafsa

Few travellers stop in Gafsa, most continuing to the more famous oases of Nefta and Tozeur. For those who have the time, however, Gafsa merits a brief visit. Located right in the centre of town, just beyond Avenue Habib Bourguiba, are two well-preserved Roman pools, each about 10sq m (12sq yds), lined with stone and with

Kebili

Until the 19th century, Kebili, the main oasis south of Chott el-Jerid, was well known for its slave market. The town's main interest to tourists is the hotel, the Borj des Autruches (Ostriches' Fort), set on the edge of the desert, with fine romantic views. Its name originates from a long-gone ostrich-breeding centre.
89km (55 miles) southeast of Tozeur, 27km (17 miles) north of Douz.

Metlaoui and Selja Gorge

Metlaoui is a dusty phosphate-mining settlement of little interest to tourists. However, it is from here that you can board the Lézard Rouge (Red Lizard)

for an unforgettable train journey deep into the heart of the Selja Gorge. The *bey* once owned the train, which was built in 1904. Although it is not in the best condition, it is still equipped with enough oriental trimmings to make a great journey even more exotic. As you pass gently through the gorge, the red ochre cliffs rise sheer to over 100m (330ft) on either side, while far below in the river, isolated palms form small pockets of greenery. It is almost as if the Lézard Rouge has left Tunisia and entered the American West. The journey can take 90 minutes.

Selja itself, in the middle of the gorge, is the halfway stop. It is from here that the best walks can be enjoyed, from the signal box to view the remarkable bridges and tunnels that the French built for the phosphate-carrying trains. Worn by the river over thousands of years, the sides of the gorge are almost sheer in places.
The Lézard Rouge office is in Metlaoui. Tel: (076) 241 469. Train journeys depart at around 10.30–11am on Tue, Thur, Fri and Sun (although times can vary). 42km (26 miles) southwest of Gafsa, 51km (32 miles) northeast of Tozeur.

Preparations for Douz's annual Festival of the Sahara

The ship of the desert

Camels are among the most exotic of animals because we associate them with the sandy desert. They conjure up romantic images of a silhouetted camel train riding into a great Saharan sunset. This can be a reality in Tunisia, as you can go on long camel treks into the desert lasting several days or just take a trip for an hour or so at somewhere like Douz. You can also go for camel rides along the beaches at most resorts in Tunisia, but nothing beats a ride on a camel in the true desert. For children this can

Sunset camel rides can be taken from Douz

An honest camel?

be the memory of a lifetime, not just of a holiday.

The camel is remarkable for its ability to survive without water for long periods. Some camels can survive for up to two weeks without drinking, but they can drink up to 130 litres (229 pints) at one time. In addition to being beasts of burden, their milk is much valued, and they are occasionally slaughtered for their meat, which is eaten on special feast days.

The desert nomad has up to 100 words to describe the camel, with different words for females, adolescents, their physical features and their personalities and moods. The camel is notorious for being a stubborn and cantankerous creature, but this is not always the case and it is usually adolescent males that are the most difficult to train and handle.

The nomads, however, have great control of their animals and know them very well, down to each animal's individual foibles. Some hold that if a camel is bad this reflects the badness in its owner. An honest man will have an honest camel.

Midès

Midès is the most spectacular of Tunisia's three famous mountain oases (the others being Tamerza and Chebika). The old village is in a perilous condition, clinging to the edge of a dramatic gorge, and most of the villagers have moved into new Midès, a collection of breeze-block huts. A defiant few remain in the old part, and recently turned down an approach by a Belgian company who wished to convert much of the place into a tourist hotel. The Tunisian tourist board, realising the value of Midès as it is, has now put a conservation order on the ancient mud-brick houses and is restoring many of them.

5km (3 miles) west of Tamerza.

Nefta

The picturesque oasis of Nefta lies on the northern edge of Chott el-Jerid. With a string of low-rise hotels, it has become a popular tourist destination on the edge of the Sahara.

Below the escarpment on which the town sits is a deep basket-shaped depression known in French as La Corbeille (The Basket) and in Arabic as Qasr el-Aïn (Castle of the Springs). La Corbeille is filled with dense clusters of palm trees, beneath which are scores of

Kebili's Borj des Autruches

THE THREE OASES

The three villages of Midès, Tamerza and Chebika lay on the main east–west caravan route, and until as recently as the 19th century derived their livelihood from this passing trade. After the caravan trade declined, the villagers became primarily dependent on their oasis gardens, sharing their produce and bartering for other goods. Besides date palms, the palm-grove gardens grow beans, chickpeas, figs, pomegranates, oranges, lemons and chillies. Tourism now supplements the villagers' livelihoods.

springs (said to total 152). These bubble up into delectable pools that are traditionally the bathing place for women and children.

A secondary pool, created by the Romans further downstream, is reserved for men and boys. The water flows on down and disappears into the main Nefta oasis. La Corbeille is barred to cars, but you can explore it on foot or by donkey.

As you stroll along Nefta's smaller side streets, you can still find, mixed in with the ever-increasing numbers of breeze-block horrors, some examples of authentic oasis architecture. These comprise low houses built of sand bricks with ornamental geometric patterns on the walls, a style found only in this region (and also in Tozeur) and in parts of Iran.

Among the sand-coloured houses you will notice the many whitewashed domes of Sufi shrines where saints are buried. Nefta is the region's religious centre and there are a hundred such shrines, plus a further 24 mosques. The two most revered shrines are the Zaouia al-Qadriya, on the ridge above La Corbeille, and the Koubba of Sidi Bou Ali, down in the main oasis. However, neither are open to non-Muslims.

Finally, don't leave Nefta without tasting its famous dates, reputed to be the finest in the region, and said to have been first planted by the town's Sufi founder, Moroccan-born Sidi Bou Ali el-Nefti, in the 13th century. The tourist office can arrange fixed-price tours of the oasis by camel (the most expensive), by donkey (the cheapest) and by pony and trap.

23km (14½ miles) southwest of Tozeur, 93km (58 miles) southwest of Gafsa.

Tamerza

The most attractive of the mountain oases is Tamerza. The town is unusual in that it caters for the high-end tourist market, as it has a luxury hotel overlooking the river and the old ghost town. The new town of Tamerza is something of a sprawl. The derelict mud-brick settlement of the old town was abandoned in 1969 after torrential rainfall and flash floods washed whole sections of it away. However, crossing the river and exploring its empty streets and alleys makes for a picturesque walk, especially in the evening. The simple buildings look much the same as they would have done in biblical times, and conservation work is under way to

The abandoned village of Old Tamerza, destroyed by flash floods

prevent the rest of the village from disintegrating.

From the new town, follow the sign down to the cascades, which are Tamerza's other main attraction. You have to walk through the primitive bamboo huts of the Hôtel des Cascades and past its swimming pool to reach the top of the waterfall, which is an attractive spot out of season, but unpleasantly infested and fly-ridden in the summer months. The souvenir shops sell such delights as pickled snakes and scorpions caught in the vicinity.

65km (40 miles) north of Tozeur.

Tozeur

This is the region's main oasis. Tozeur's old quarter is famous for the brick architecture of its alleys and passageways, decorated with the lozenges, zigzags and chevrons that are also found on the locally made Berber rugs. Tozeur's main attraction is its oasis, which is growing as a result of reclamation projects on the edge of the *chott*. Horse-drawn carriages offer tours of the palm grove and of two small zoos. The first zoo, with ostriches, a boar, a hyena, a pair of lions, owls, eagles and peacocks, is within the aptly named Paradise Gardens. This colourful and exotic park, halfway round the palm-grove tour, has pathways lined with fragrant flowers and shaded by palms and fruit trees. The second zoo, the Si Tijani Zoo, open daily from 8am to 6pm, is well signposted and has a fine collection of local animals.

The town's other attraction is the Dar Cheriat Museum, built in traditional style, with a collection of folk exhibits and local costumes together with souvenir shops. Beyond the Dar Cheriat a path leads to a rocky outcrop known as the Belvedere, which offers extensive views over the palm grove. The palm grove itself has natural hot springs where women bathe in the morning, and men in the afternoon. The springs are used mainly by local people,

although a few intrepid foreigners sometimes venture in.

23km (14½ miles) northeast of Nefta, 93km (58 miles) southwest of Gafsa.

Traditional brickwork pattern

The distinctive brickwork patterns found in the Tozeur region are repeated in the local rugs

Walk: Tamerza to Midès

One of the most scenic and romantic spots in the country, the river and gorge between Tamerza and Midès make an excellent walk. More robust visitors can ride there on a donkey if they prefer. Avoid the midday period between 11am and 3pm in the summer months, as the gorge can be very hot, with no wind.

It is essential to take your own water. If you opt for the donkey ride, be aware that you will be very sore for a couple of days afterwards. The trip is best arranged from the Tamerza Palace Hotel or the Hôtel des Cascades, and can be set up at just a few hours' notice.

Starting at the Tamerza Palace Hotel, the donkeys follow a trail over the ridge opposite Tamerza's old ghost town, then cut across a flat open plain to approach Midès from the same direction as the tarmacked road. They reach new Midès beside the customs

A little haven of peace and tranquillity at Tamerza

The waterfall (Cascades) at Tamerza still flows, even at the height of summer

post (Algeria is just over the next hill), with old Midès beyond, at the opposite end of the oasis.

The walking route from the Tamerza Palace Hotel along the river is more scenic and dramatic than the donkey route. Where the tarmacked road from Tamerza to Tozeur crosses the river, you must fork to the right into the gorge.

This gorge is known as Oued el-Oudei and it becomes increasingly scenic and ever narrower. As it twists and turns, you have a wonderful sense of entering another world, devoid of cars, telephones and all other man-made inventions.

Your first sight of Midès, perched precariously on the ridge of a vertical rock face surrounded by the gorge on three sides, is breathtaking. If you dare look down into the gorge, you'll see a swirling multicoloured cross-section of browns, beiges and russet-coloured rock strata, with dots of palm green deep in the valley below. You have a sense of disturbing the peace when you arrive, and the villagers have only recently discovered the evils of money, previously relying entirely on barter for their daily needs. In the centre of Midès, a few of the simple one-room houses have now become discreet souvenir shops, selling local produce like dates and oranges, together with petrified wood and mineral rocks.

The palm grove, which is the villagers' livelihood, is behind Midès. Here towering date palms give shade to pomegranate, fig, lemon and orange trees, as well as chilli plants, chickpeas and beans. Each villager has a small parcel of land and the water from the springs is shared meticulously.

Jerba and the south

Southern Tunisia is the heart of Berber country. With the developing resort of Jerba, its crumbling but magnificent ksour, *its underground dwellings at Matmata and the desolate, rocky edges of the Sahara, it is a land of contrasts. Town settlements are built along the natural contours of barren mountain ridges.*

In complete contrast to these mountains is the Île de Jerba in the south, the legendary 'Island of the Lotos-Eaters' that no one ever wants to leave. This holiday paradise, which is totally flat and with plenty of sunshine, is the only place in Tunisia where you can swim in the sea well into the winter months.

Olive trees are hardy enough to survive even in the south of Tunisia

Jerba is the obvious base for exploring the south. At least a week is needed here for a proper balance between tours into the interior and time spent lazing on the beach. Two day-trips are highly recommended: one to the Matmata troglodytic cave region, the other a circuit of the Berber fortress villages to the south. Note that in July and August temperatures reach 40°C (104°F) and skins will roast in the Saharan heat.

Historically, the dominant feature in this region has been perpetual intertribal conflict between settled farmers and raiding nomads. Indigenous Berbers who cultivated and irrigated their oases and orchards have long had to contend with invading nomadic Arab tribes who burnt and destroyed their crops to make pastureland for their herds. Of all parts of Tunisia, this has always been the most lawless and violent, and 18th- and 19th-century foreign travellers avoided going there. Today, however, you should encounter no such problem.

JERBA

Jerba is joined to the mainland by a man-made causeway called El-Kantara (The Bridge). This is the legendary Land of the Lotos-Eaters described in Homer's *Odyssey* and in which Odysseus and his crew were distracted from their voyage by tasting the

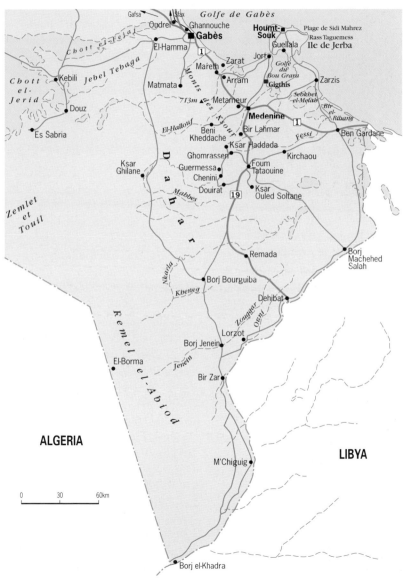

Pots for catching octopus, Houmt-Souk harbour

complex irrigation system, catching the scant rainfall and using the wells to tap the slightly salty groundwater. Drinking water is piped across from the mainland but the island's own water supplies are sufficient for the cultivation of olive, fig and palm trees. The Phoenicians introduced metalworking, weaving, dyeing and pottery-making, trades that continue on the island today. Jerba has remained relatively independent, being administered by the mainland only since 1604.

Houmt-Souk

Jerba's major town, Houmt-Souk, literally meaning 'market quarter', is the island's 'capital'. With several whitewashed squares lined with attractive arcades draped with purple bougainvillaea, the town has distinctive architecture. The Jerbans have always spread themselves out, with each family living on its agricultural smallholding. Less than a quarter of the island's population is therefore concentrated in Houmt-Souk, and the town as a result still retains an uncluttered, open feel. A stroll through the markets of Houmt-Souk is a pleasant experience, with no sense of bustle or hassle.

delights of the lotus fruit. It is thought that they imbibed a Jerban date-palm-sap liqueur called *laghmi*. Ulysses had difficulty getting all his crew on board afterwards and the descendants of these castaways are reputed to be living on Jerba today.

Jerba is the only place in Tunisia that can truly be called a year-round tourist destination, although even here it is chilly from November through to January. The main stretch of tourist development is along the sandy Plage de Sidi Mahares on the northeast coast. Jerba makes a good base from which to explore the Berber villages, the Matmata troglodytic dwellings, Chott el-Jerid and its oases, Tozeur and Nefta.

For Jerba's islanders, life is far from idyllic as the fertility of their farms is sustained only by continual labour on a

There are two other main sights in Houmt-Souk: the Museum of Popular Arts and Traditions, in an 18th-century *zaouia*, where Jerban costumes, pottery and jewellery are displayed, and Borj el-Kebir, a 15th-century fortress on the eastern end of the port,

with a colossal gateway flanked
by cannons.

Museum of Popular Arts and Traditions.
Open: Sat–Thur 9am–noon, 2–6.30pm
in summer, 2–5.30pm in winter.
Borj el-Kebir. Open: daily 8am–noon,
2–5pm. Admission charge. 45km
(28 miles) north of Zarzis.

RELIGION ON JERBA

Jerba also differs from the Tunisian mainland
for two religious reasons. It is the home of an
Islamic sect known as the Kharijites and of
most of Tunisia's Jewish community. The
Kharijites, whose religion is outside
mainstream Islamic faith, took refuge here
in the 10th century, to escape persecution
by orthodox Muslims. While the Berbers of
Jerba remained faithful to the Aghlabid view
of Islam, the rest of the country adopted
the Fatimid creed that swept in from Egypt
in the 10th century. The Kharijites are also
known for their austerity and their extremely
simple mosques, of which there are about 300
on the island.

Jerba is also home to a prominent Jewish
community. Although many Jerban Jews
emigrated to Israel in 1948, about 1,000
remain and continue their tradition of
jewellery-making. Island synagogues are open
to the public. The most famous and most
visited is the El-Griba Synagogue (The
Marvellous), one of the holiest Jewish sites in
North Africa. The original synagogue was
founded in 600 BC when, according to legend,
a holy stone fell from heaven, indicating the
site. The current synagogue dates only from
1920 but it is a handsome building with dark
wood panelling, stained glass and ornate tiles.
Visitors are welcome at all times except
Saturday mornings, when Sabbath prayers are
said. Tragically, the synagogue was subjected
to a terrorist truck bomb in April 2002, when
19 people were killed.

The Strangers' Mosque at Houmt-Souk, Jerba

Guellala

On the island's south coast, Guellala is
Jerba's capital of pottery. The town is
famed for its pottery stores, and there is
not much else to do here except shop. If
you want to buy a decorated plate, this
is the place to go for the best price.

KSOUR
Chenini

With its dramatic location, Chenini is
the best-known and most visited of the
Berber village strongholds. If you visit
independently, you can avoid most of
the summer congestion by taking the
unpaved track to the left (which forks
off at the foot of the spur) before the
tarmacked road rounds the corner to
the centre of the village. This track
zigzags up through the village houses,
culminating at a whitewashed mosque
near the summit of the fortified ridge.
From here you can walk to the highest

The old town of Douirat clings to the rock face

point of the ridge and enjoy excellent views down over the houses and dwellings that lie in the horseshoe-shape of the mountainside. The old brick-built houses on the upper slope, some of which date from the 12th century, are now entirely derelict, but many of the lower cave dwellings or houses are still inhabited. Follow the path round the lower houses to a second abandoned village, set along

A TALL STORY

According to legend, the room with the overlong graves in the underground mosque at Chenini is the place where Roman soldiers buried seven Christians alive. They slept for 400 years and grew to twice their original height. On awakening they were made to convert to Islam so that they could die a normal, peaceful death.

the escarpment where an underground mosque still survives (*see box*).
18km (11 miles) west of Foum Tataouine, 20km (12½ miles) northeast of Douirat.

Douirat

This fortified village perched dramatically on a 700m (2,297ft) high peak dominates the landscape. A whitewashed mosque stands out from the other stone buildings, which are cut into the sand-coloured stone of the rock face. Unlike Chenini, Douirat is not on the Berber village tourist circuit, and is therefore much less visited. The old village is now mostly unoccupied thanks to the new settlement built down below in the 1960s. The *ghar* (caves) were known to have housed over 5,000 inhabitants right up until

the 19th century. The women that remain are extremely wary of foreign visitors, so use your camera very discreetly, if at all. The mosque here has the only known archaic Berber inscription inside it, though no one can decipher what it says, and non-Muslims are not permitted to see it.
13km (8 miles) southwest of Foum Tataouine.

Foum Tataouine

Foum Tataouine means 'Mouth of the Springs' in Berber and it is, of course, the place where Luke Skywalker lived. It is Tunisia's southernmost tourist base, but there is little of interest here despite the fact the final scene of *The X-Files* was shot here.

Built by the French administrators, the town still has the feel of a colonial outpost, with one wide, palm-lined main boulevard – another Avenue Habib Bourguiba (of course) – and sandy streets leading off it. The French used Foum Tataouine as a garrison town, with a military base here. On Mondays and Thursdays the market is a lively spectacle, with sheep, olives and locally-made blankets the major things

Donkeys are laden with plastic containers with water from the village well at Chenini

on sale, although the main interest to tourists is in observing the range of local people who are drawn in from outlying villages and nomad camps. A local delicacy of the town is *kab el-ghazal* or *corne de gazelle* (gazelle's horn), a horn-shaped pastry filled with nuts and honey.

120km (75 miles) south of Gabès.

Ghomrassen

Set in a steep valley, Ghomrassen is the largest settlement in this typical Berber area. Inhabited cave dwellings (*ghars*) with very simple single rooms, a cooking area in front and a living area raised up behind, are still to be found here, though most are now dangerous because of rock falls from the cliffs.

Beyond Ghomrassen, on the road back to Foum Tataouine, stands a prominent *ksar*. You can drive in and tour its impressive courtyards, now deserted but still in good condition.

24km (15 miles) northwest of Foum Tataouine.

Guermessa

The most haunting of the cliff-top Berber villages and – built about 800 years ago – also the oldest, Guermessa is clearly visible from the main road, although stamina and perseverance are needed to explore it. The modern settlement at its foot has drawn most of the villagers away, although a few still prefer to remain up on the cliff top despite the relative hardship and absence of sanitation and electricity.

Mosque and Sidi Moussa Ben Abdullah *marabout*, Ghomrassen

Cut directly into the barren ridge, the windows of the houses look like hundreds of eyes watching your every move as you approach. The villagers will assure you that the ascent takes a mere 15 minutes. Visitors, however, should allow an hour or more.

18km (11 miles) west of Foum Tataouine.

Ksar Haddada

This small settlement, just a few kilometres north of Ghomrassen, is famous for its excellently restored *ksar*. The town may be marked on some

maps as Ghomrassen-Haddada. The maze of little steps, courtyards and roof terraces are great fun to explore, especially for children. In its heyday the *ksar* was used as a food store by four local tribes, the Haddada, the Hamdoun from Ghomrassen and two other local tribes claiming Libyan and Moroccan origins. It is one of the locations that was chosen for filming certain episodes of *Star Wars*.
25km (15¹/₂ miles) northwest of Foum Tataouine, 5km (3 miles) north of Ghomrassen.

Ksar Ouled Soltane

The best-preserved of Tunisia's *ksour*, Ouled Soltane has two courtyards with *ghorfas* (rooms) still standing up to four storeys high and its outer wall is in excellent condition. The *ksar* continues to be used as a store for grain and olives, and by virtue of its relative isolation it is still fully used by the local community, whose lifestyle has not altered greatly in recent centuries. After Friday prayers the two courtyards serve as the debating and meeting place for the semi-nomadic Ouled Chehida tribe, who are based here but who also spend periods of time in the pastures with their sheep, goats and camels. This *ksar* hosts a local festival in late November.
19km (12 miles) south of Foum Tataouine.

Remada

Tunisia's southernmost town, Remada is a small oasis where the Romans constructed a minor fort and the French incorporated the remains of it into a garrison town. Today the place still exists for essentially military reasons, as the first line of defence against Libya. Dehibat, to the southeast, is the southernmost crossing point into Libya for civilians. The vast tracts of land further south, towards the point of Tunisia's southernmost triangle, are strictly closed to visitors. The special permits needed to enter this zone are unlikely to be granted. Borj Bourguiba, to the southwest, is a simple settlement with a military prison, where Habib Bourguiba (*see p71*), who later became President, was interned by the French during the Protectorate years.
70km (43 miles) south of Foum Tataouine.

KSAR AND KSOUR

A *ksar* (plural *ksour*) is a fortified granary, typical of certain regions of North Africa. Small villages grew up around these granaries, which are generally located on a hilltop for additional protection. These mud and stone structures are an unmistakable architectural peculiarity of the Berber south. *Ksour* have several simple barrel-vaulted rooms (*ghorfas*). The *ghorfas* were built side by side and on top of one another, usually stacked three or four high. Each *ghorfa* is connected to the others by interior or exterior stairs. The Berbers built these *ksour* to protect their food stocks from the invading Arab armies. *Ksour* also fulfilled the function of fortified towns, presenting their high, windowless façades to the outside world. Some of the best examples of *ksour* can be seen at Medenine, Ksar Haddada and Ksar Ouled Soltane.

The Berbers

As an ethnic group, the Tunisian Berbers, the indigenous inhabitants of the south, are on the verge of extinction, as they become increasingly absorbed by the dominant Arab culture. This process of absorption has been a long and gradual one, starting with the Arab conquest of Tunisia in the 7th century. Earlier, under the Romans, Berber had been Tunisia's main language, but Arabic, the language of the new religion of Islam, soon took over. By the end of the 19th century, only the inhabitants of the three key villages in the Berber heartlands – Chenini, Douirat and Guermessa – still used Berber as their first language.

Today, just a few elderly women continue to speak Berber, the men having migrated to the cities in search of work and higher wages, returning only for a few weeks of the year. The women make a meagre living from weaving rugs, while the young men move to Tunis or Sousse. Some still return, using their savings to pay the local price for a *pride* (dowry) or to buy livestock or land. However, many more emigrate to France or Libya. As it ages, the community left behind is dying out.

The most enduring testament to Tunisian Berber culture is the collection of village strongholds built on the barren ridges of the south, most notably in the Jebel Demer mountain range just west of Foum Tataouine. Douirat, one of the larger

Uncertain future for young and old

Berber villages, has a population of over 2,000. More usually a village has only 40 or 50 families, with one elected *shaikh* (headman).

Berber communities are traditionally based on agriculture, involving the tending of *jessour* (terraces) and managing water resources by means of cisterns and careful irrigation. However, the invasion of the Arab tribes from the 7th century onwards drove the Berbers off their carefully tended plains and forced them up into these dramatic crags in order to survive. Because the desert climate made conventional agriculture so difficult, with perhaps only one good grain crop every few years, it was essential to defend the village granaries (*ksour*) from attack and plunder by other tribes.

A Berber camp with donkeys out grazing

Matmata and Gabès

The alien world around Matmata was used as a setting for the film Star Wars: A New Hope *and it is no surprise. The underground homes of the locals look like they are from another planet.*

Matmata

With its troglodytic dwellings, the weird moonscape of Matmata is one of the highlights of any visit to Tunisia. If possible, you should experience a night in one of the converted cave hotels known as *hôtels troglodytiques*.

The first thing you notice when you arrive at Matmata is the strangely barren, eroded landscape, with hills

Some troglodyte villagers make their living from inviting tourists to visit

that look almost manufactured. Then you gradually begin to notice a few caves cut into the hillsides that look as if they are used for keeping livestock rather than for human habitation. The road climbs higher and signs implore you to '*Visitez Maison Troglodyte*', as tracks lead off to what seems to be nothing at all. The road then passes over the brow of the hill and drops down into a sort of natural bowl with a few, modern, brick buildings scattered here and there and hundreds of circular craters, each some 10m (11yds) in diameter.

About 5,000 people live in Matmata, a proportion of them in the 700 cave and crater houses (*see p131*). The town is also the centre for the Hammama des Matmata tribe. These Berbers were mentioned in ancient times as raiders on the southern fringes of the Roman Empire.

Foum Tataouine got the name fame, but Matmata got the film crews. Ever since the town was used as a setting for

Star Wars, the number of tourists who come here has rocketed. Most arrive from the coastal resorts in time for lunch, so that by 4pm the town tends to have emptied again, which is a good reason for visiting either early in the morning or in the late afternoon, even spending the night here.

Half of Matmata's 700 underground homes are still inhabited. Some inhabitants resent the tourists' intrusion to the extent that they have put barbed wire round their courtyards to keep unwanted visitors at bay. So don't go snooping around uninvited and respect people's privacy. Others, however, make a living by inviting tourists in to look around their homes.

Since the 1960s the three largest sets of underground complexes have been converted into hotels, which are interesting to visit, if only for a drink in the courtyard. The Marhala Hotel, run by the Touring Club de Tunisie, is probably the most attractive and pleasant, with three courtyards linked by underground corridors, and 100 beds ranged in 36 cell-like rooms. The more famous, the Hotel Sidi Driss, is a magnet for bus-tour visitors and it gets very crowded during the day.

A local *souk* is held in Matmata on Mondays and an annual festival, with folk dancing and music, in November. If you have the time to see some more troglodytic houses, visit El-Haddej, just off the main road north of Matmata, where the villagers are much less inundated with tourists. In the past, El-Haddej was much larger than Matmata, but heavy floods in 1969 devastated many of its homes. It was the location for some of the scenes from *Monty Python's Life of Brian*.

At Tijma, 4km (2½ miles) north of Matmata on route 107, is the Maison

A typical troglodyte dwelling

Fatima. A talismanic fishtail hangs above the entrance to the house. This is an established tourist shop where the people are friendly, relaxed and pleased to show you their humble abode.

Gabès

Although it is a coastal oasis, Gabès is not the prettiest of towns. It is highly industrialised and has serious pollution problems, so, apart from its palm grove, it is of limited interest to tourists. No trace of the town's Carthaginian or Roman past remains, and little from its heyday in the 9th to 11th centuries, when it was a walled city thriving on the caravan route across the Sahara and to Mecca. Within the borders of Gabès are three villages – Menzel, Jara and Chenini (a different town from the one mentioned on p122). Jara is the most picturesque, with an old quarter near the riverbank, and the narrow, cobbled streets in the market are lined with basketwork and woven palm items, set out for sale.

On the edge of town, in an exquisite 17th-century marble *madrasa*, is the Museum of Arts and Popular Traditions. Beside the museum is the mosque and tomb of Sidi Boulbaba, barber of the Prophet Muhammad and believed to have been the founder of Arab Gabès in the 7th century. This is still a popular place of pilgrimage.

The oasis palm grove, with an estimated 300,000 date palms, is at its most picturesque at Chenini, and is sufficiently well established as a tourist

destination for there to be horse-drawn carriages waiting beyond the bus station to take visitors on the standard tour. Here you can see how a typical oasis works, with date palms sheltering fig and olive trees, below which grow vines, corn, vegetables and grass. If you don't want to ride you can stroll along the sandy paths, but as most of the fields have high fences of palm fronds you won't see much. The ride ends at a café beside the remains of a Roman dam, next door to which is a rather unlikely crocodile farm and a zoo. A path leads on past the Chella Club Hotel, and beyond to some fine gorges at the very edge of the oasis.

Museum of Arts and Popular Traditions.
Open: Tue–Sun 9am–noon, 2–5pm.
Admission charge.
252km (157 miles) south of Tunis,
136km (85 miles) south of Sfax.

A circuit of the Gabès oasis palmery by *calèche* (horse-drawn carriage)

Troglodytic caves

Most of the Tunisian troglodytic caves (cave dwellings) are in the area around Matmata. The Tunisian troglodytic tradition is centuries old, with some caves inhabited for 400 years. However, the most famous cave dwellings at Matmata date only from the 19th century.

In the past, the local people began living in rock-cut caves not only because it was easier to burrow into the soft, crumbly tufa than to use it for building, but also because the temperature underground was far more equable than above; it was cooler in summer, and warmer in winter. Some troglodytic caves were built for defensive reasons and their camouflaged appearance still makes them difficult to detect. In the rare instance of heavy rainfall, flash floods can cause great problems and even make troglodytic caves collapse. This is what happened in Haddej in the late 1960s.

The layout of these underground houses follows the typical Arab or North African model. There is a *haouch* (central open courtyard), about 10m deep and 10–15m wide (33 × 33–49ft). Off this central courtyard are the traditional four rooms, one for eating, one for sleeping, one for stabling, one for storage of such staple foods as grain and olives, and for animal fodder. The rooms tend to be the same size, and a richer man will simply extend the number of his courtyards rather than increase the size of his rooms. The largest dwellings have two or three such courtyards, most of which have now been converted into tourist hotels. A gently sloping entrance tunnel, large enough for a camel, connects the floor of the main courtyard to ground level. The storerooms frequently have holes in the ceiling for pouring supplies in directly from above.

A night spent by candlelight in one of the simply furnished cave bedrooms of the troglodytic hotels will give you a real impression of life underground.

Interior of a troglodyte house

Drive: Matmata to the coast

This drive takes you through some rarely visited villages of the south. There are no facilities en route for refreshment, so make sure you are sufficiently well equipped with your own food and water. The entire route is on tarmacked roads, but if you accidentally stray from the route (the signposting is confusing and often in Arabic) you could end up on a piste (unmetalled track). The quality of the roads in this area of Tunisia is unpredictable, so carry enough water with you in case you get a puncture, your hire car breaks down or you end up going the wrong way.

Allow 2 to 3 hours for the trip.

1 Matmata
Starting in Matmata, head north towards Gabès on the main road. After about 12km (7½ miles) you can make a detour off the road for Matmata el-Jedid.

2 Matmata el-Jedid
This is an optional detour. Although it is an unexciting breeze-block settlement on a flat plain, Matmata el-Jedid gives an idea of how tough living

in this area can be. This is where many of the original local inhabitants have relocated, moving into houses with modern facilities such as running water, plumbing, electricity and television. *From Matmata el-Jedid head south again along the 107 to Matmata and then towards Medenine on route 104. The scenery on this road is dramatic.*

3 Toujane
Set in a photogenic gorge, this is one of the most spectacularly located towns in Tunisia. Mud-block houses cling to the hillside below a *kasbah* while a white mosque stands as a sentinel to Islam. *From Toujane take the road north to Aïn Tounine. You leave route 104 to Medenine.*

4 Aïn Tounine
This is a small and remote village. The road takes you straight

through the market square, a vast mud courtyard surrounded by workshops, each trade grouped together, with a wonderful mud hut for the village coffee house.

From Aïn Tounine follow the signposts to Mareth. The road heads first back towards Matmata Nouvelle.

fertile valleys, which in contrast to the rather barren landscapes of Matmata itself, are densely wooded. The trees are remarkably diverse, with several species besides palms.

Continue along the road to Matmata Nouvelle until a right turn branches off in the direction of Mareth.

5 Bení Zelten

Bení Zelten itself is a striking village, unusually ranged out over a hillside, beneath the ruins of a hilltop fort. Most of the houses are built in the local brown stone, and many are derelict, having been abandoned by the villagers in favour of the breeze-block houses of Matmata el-Jedid. Among the old houses on the hillside are a number of cave dwellings; some are still in use, while others lie deserted.

The narrow tarmacked road continues through increasingly attractive countryside, with surprisingly

6 Mareth

The road winds through some very pretty scenery. Keep your eyes open for any black tents on the side of the roadside. These are the dwellings of the local tribespeople who still maintain their nomadic lifestyle, taking their flocks of sheep, camels and goats to graze on widely dispersed pastureland. It comes as something of a shock when, from this world from a bygone era, you suddenly emerge onto the busy main Gabès–Medenine road. You have just glimpsed an aspect of Tunisia that is seldom seen.

Straight roads are a feature of the south, like this one to Matmata el-Jedid

MEDENINE

Medenine is bisected by a river, the Oued Medenine. This is the origin of its name, which means 'two towns' in Arabic. The French used Medenine as their southern headquarters, and it was the main market centre for southern Tunisia's produce. Over the last 100 years, the condition of the *ksar*, off the Rue des Palmiers in the centre of Medenine, has slowly deteriorated.

Intriguing modern design and sculpture at Medenine

It was originally a large, six-storey building, but all that now remains is a large courtyard. The *ghorfas* around the courtyard have been converted into souvenir shops bedecked with Berber carpets for the benefit of coach tours. Behind this courtyard are more *ghorfas*, which are now derelict, although some are up to three storeys high. Today grain is stored not in the *ksar* but in conventional silos on the outskirts of town.

73km (45 miles) south of Gabès.

METAMEUR

This small town, in a flat river valley, lies just north of Medenine. The population all around is semi-nomadic, and on Fridays people arrive here from the surrounding grazing land to attend noon-day prayers and catch up on the local gossip. The town's 600-year-old *ksar* is its most prominent feature, the building's remarkably well-preserved silhouette rising above the plain. The *ksar* has three courtyards which rise three storeys high. An enterprising and knowledgeable Berber has converted its best-preserved section into a basic hotel suitable for those seeking an 'authentic' Tunisian experience.

6km (3½ miles) northwest of Medenine.

GIGTHIS

As it is not comparable to the Roman sites of the north like Dougga and Thuburbo Majus, few tourists go to Gigthis. Under Roman rule, it was one of Africa's major ports and later

The old *ksar* and the new mosque sit side by side at Metameur

became a major trading port on the trans-Saharan caravan routes. The Arabs destroyed it when they invaded Tunisia in the 7th century and the site remained forgotten until excavations uncovered it in 1906.

Present-day Gigthis enjoys a pleasant seaside setting, and its most impressive remains are the large forum built in Hadrian's reign (AD 117–138). It has green fluted columns and is dominated by a temple of Serapis and Isis. A paved road leads down to the port, which silted up long ago, although an ancient stone jetty is still just visible. The baths beside the forum have a few remnants of mosaic flooring.

42km (26 miles) south of Houmt-Souk.
Open: daily 8am–6pm.
Admission charge.

ZARZIS

Zarzis has prospered and expanded because of the excellent sandy beaches on its northern side, where package hotels have sprung up. The town itself was established by the French as a garrison town (still with barracks) and it has almost nothing of interest to visitors except a signpost announcing 'Cairo 2,591km' (1,610 miles). On its edge are plantations of palm and olive trees.
20km (12½ miles) southeast of Jerba.

Getting away from it all

For the adventurous spirit, there is no greater thrill than heading out into the desert wilderness and camping out under the stars. Transport modes vary from the comfort of a four-wheel-drive to horses, or bouncing atop a camel. Hikers should head to one of the National Parks.

4WD Desert Safaris

Viewed from the comfort of a four-star hotel on the coast, the attractions of a three- or four-day safari excursion may seem very alluring. In a relatively short space of time they offer a taste of the Tunisian interior with its desert and mountain oases. However, it is essential to realise that these excursions cover a huge amount of terrain in a short period, and often involve 5.30am departures, with long spells on the road in bumpy, uncomfortable Land Rovers that are filled to capacity. The time actually spent at any of the destinations is fairly minimal and those in search of a deeper experience of the interior are likely to be disappointed.

Desert safaris are at their best between October and April, when the

Reach inaccessible spots in an off-roader

Land Rovers are the favoured vehicle for 4WD excursions into the desert

heat of the desert is less intense. From June to August, when temperatures at midday soar into the 40s (30s F), it can be unbearably hot, so that few find it an enjoyable experience.

A four-wheel-drive vehicle is required to make the journey to Ksar Ghilane, a Roman fort on the edge of the desert, which is signposted from the Douirat-to-Chenini track. Running for a distance of 47km (29 miles) on desert track, this route passes through the arid desert landscapes of the Dahar plateau, but there is the possibility of spotting desert gazelles and antelopes. Jeep tours come here from Gabès or from Douz, and traditional Berber-style tents are set up close to the sand-drenched walls of the fort.

You will also need four-wheel-drive transport for the trek along the floor of the canyon between Tamerza and Midès. The route follows a sandy

riverbed, but at certain times of year it involves crossing some streams. If you hire a four-wheel-drive vehicle independently, make sure that you are aware of the 'rules' of driving in this part of the world, and that you go well equipped. The golden rules are:

• Always have at least 5 litres (9 pints) of water per person on board, and carry extra non-perishable food rations like biscuits, chocolate and processed cheese.

• Should you get caught up in a sandstorm, stop and point your vehicle downwind to minimise damage to the engine and windscreen.

• Don't attempt to go off-road unless there is more than one vehicle in your group. There should always be at least two vehicles together.

• If you drive over sand, it is essential to maintain a sufficient speed so as not to get bogged down. If you get stuck in sand, the best way to get out is with a set of two sand ladders, short metal ladders that are placed under the front or back wheels that will allow you to manoeuvre the vehicle out of the sand. The jolting that this entails is considerable and may well loosen the vehicle's bolts or even its welded joints, so make sure that the undercarriage is properly checked after a desert trip. Also remember that petrol consumption when driving in sand is very high because the engine is in low gears, so always ensure that you have adequate supplies in spare cans.

• Inform the Garde Nationale at the nearest town to your journey, to make sure that the authorities are aware of your destination and proposed route.

• Finally, and most importantly, should you break down or get lost, always stay with your vehicle. A person wandering alone in the desert is infinitely more difficult to find than a car.

Camel treks

Camel treks are only for the young and fit and those who are seriously committed to having a more genuine experience of the desert. You should be aware, too, that the amount of ground covered by camel is obviously only a tiny fraction of what can be travelled in a four-wheel-drive vehicle. But the advantage of a camel trek is that you will see one small area in depth and at a leisurely pace rather than covering a large area at speed.

The main centres for camel treks are Douz, Nefta and Tozeur. The tourist offices here organise trips, which range from one hour to 10 days. Douz and Ksar Metameur offer the most adventurous expeditions led by

Patiently waiting for the first tourists of the day

Café sign in southern Tunisia

experienced local guides, riding from well to well, pitching nomad tents and cooking on campfires. Some operators offer the option of moving from one *ksar* to the next and camping in simple *ghorfas* for shelter. Saddle sores are to be expected, especially on the first day or so, but most people seem to get inured after that. In addition to the tourist offices there is an excellent and enterprising firm called Camping Nomade el-Nouail at Douz, 5km (3 miles) off the road to the south. Camel treks can also be organised at El-Faouar, at the end of the tarmacked road from Douz.

For this kind of adventure, the time of year is obviously an all-important consideration. Avoid the summer, when temperatures regularly exceed 40°C (104°F) and when activity must be restricted to the early morning and the late afternoon and evening. The best times are between November and April, when you will need warm clothing for the evening, as desert temperatures can dip below 0°C (32°F).

Desert and mountain oases

Few sights are as impressive as a desert oasis. Here, amid a barren, scorched landscape of rock and dust, are springs of running water, cool pools and gardens of opulent fertility shaded by palm fronds.

Don't be deceived by the romantic imagery, however, for although you may imagine that the inhabitants of oases simply bask in the shade of their palm trees all day long, the system of irrigation and husbandry that lies behind a successful oasis settlement is extraordinarily complex. Indeed, some 19th-century French engineers who thought they could improve on the system confessed themselves baffled by its mysteries.

Date palms, luscious lifeline of the desert

In the great oases like Tozeur (*see pp114–15*) and Nefta (*see pp112–13*) the water gushing from the hundreds of springs below is distributed equally to each plot. Any salt springs must be channelled safely away from the gardens and all sewage must be regulated. The system requires constant tending and maintenance, yet there is no formal method of enforcement, only mutual trust and dependence. As you walk or ride through any oasis garden, note the number of crops. In the shade of the towering date palms, olive and fruit trees grow, and these in turn provide shade for wheat and vegetables.

Tunisia's oases are concentrated in the Chott el-Jerid region (*see p107*). The mountain oases are small and

dramatic, with clusters of palm trees bursting out from arid cliff faces and gorges. Desert oases are on an entirely different scale. Tozeur's oasis is the largest of all, covering more than 1,000 hectares (2,470 acres) and with over 300,000 trees. Nefta's 152 springs irrigate its 400,000 trees.

National parks

Since independence, Tunisia has striven to create national parks to preserve its landscapes, flora and fauna. The country now has eight national parks: Bou Hedma National Park, Boukornine National Park, Feija National Park, Jebel Chambi National Park, Jebel Ichkeul National Park, Orbata National Park, Sidi Toui Saharan National Park and Zagouan National Park.

DATE PALMS

Without date palms, the lifeline of the Sahara, the region would not be habitable. In addition to the dates themselves, the trees provide animal fodder from the stones and fibre for making rope and shoes. The best and most highly prized type of date is the *deglet en-nour* (finger of light) which is harvested in November and is found mostly in Tozeur, Nefta and Douz, (Nefta's crop is the most highly rated). There are over 100 types of date, all varying according to the climatic band they grow in. Each tree lives for 150 to 200 years and can produce 120kg (265lbs) of dates a year. Of all fruits, dates are the richest in protein and sugar. The sap of old palm trees which are no longer productive is used to make *laghmi,* a potent wine. Quite apart from the fruit and the drink, the wood of the tree is used to build houses, bridges for crossing irrigation channels and fences around fields, while the fronds are also used for fencing and for weaving baskets, mats and roofing. The *jerid* is the base of the palm and has given its name to the Chott el-Jerid region.

Bou Hedma National Park, 85km (53 miles) east of Gafsa, is a 350sq km (135sq miles) area of upland country with desert animals like gazelle and golden eagles. Jebel Chambi National Park has 600sq km (232 sq miles) of forest in the Tunisian Atlas round the country's highest mountain, with wild goats, wild pigs and moufflon. Jebel Ichkeul National Park is a 100sq km (39sq miles) area on the south side of Lake Ichkeul, near Bizerte (*see pp52–3*).

Remote inland sites

As a holidaymaker in Tunisia, getting away from other people can sometimes seem impossible. Most excursions organised from resort hotels are to well-visited towns like Kairouan and Tunis, which are invariably crowded, or to famous ruins like Dougga and Sbeïtla, where chances of avoiding coach tours are slim. For those who yearn to explore a little of Tunisia independently, it is well worth hiring a car and visiting one or more of the following sites. At all of these places refreshment facilities are

Touzeur oasis

The extensive bucolic ruins of Roman Bulla Regia are famous for their underground villas

limited or entirely lacking, so set off well equipped with your own supplies of food and drink.

Bulla Regia

Too far from the main eastern coastal resorts of Hammamet, Monastir and Sousse to be on the coach-tour route, the Roman site of Bulla Regia can only be visited on a day trip from Tabarka, or even from Tunis if a very early start is made. Bulla Regia's unique setting on the slopes of the Mejerda river valley is very attractive, but the real draw is its underground villas, which give a fascinating glimpse into daily life in Roman times (*see p50*).

Chemtou

If you have hired your own transport and have just visited Bulla Regia, go on to nearby Chemtou (*see p50*). Here are the Roman quarries from which many of Tunisia's marble statues were carved. It is approached from the track that forks west, directly opposite the point where the Bulla Regia fork bends east at the crossroads on the Jendouba road. The quarries lie in the twin-peaked hill above Chemtou. These quarries were the only source of the highly prized *antico giallo*, a honey-brown marble with dark red veins. Unfinished, half-cut columns still remain in the quarries, and above them is a hilltop sanctuary with an altar dedicated to the Phoenician god Baal Hammon.

Haïdra, Makthar and Medeina

These are three remote ancient Roman towns, smaller and less imposing than the major Roman cities of Dougga,

Sbeïtla and Thuburbo Majus, but still rewarding in their own right. Makthar (*see pp99–100*), the most accessible, impressive and best preserved of the three, can be reached on a day trip from the coastal resorts of Sousse or Monastir. The ruins cover a large area and take at least two hours to explore thoroughly. Medeina (*see pp100–3*) is further inland, but if you make a very early start, it could be incorporated into your day trip to Makthar.

Lying deep inland just a few kilometres from the Algerian border, Haïdra (*see p92*) is the remotest of all the Roman sites. As it is too far from anywhere to visit on a day trip, you will need to stay overnight either in Le Kef or Sbeïtla. Although Haïdra does not have particularly imposing monuments, it has the distinctive atmosphere of a frontier town.

Table de Jugurtha

This extraordinary table mountain near the Algerian border is one of the remotest and most exciting places in Tunisia. On the summit are a ruined village and a shrine that still attracts pilgrims. Visiting the Table de Jugurtha will be one of the most memorable highlights of your holiday (*see pp92 and 94–5*). You'll need to spend a night in Le Kef.

Zarzis has one of the largest sandy beaches in the country

Parasailing at Jerba

Surf and steam

Beaches

Tunisia enjoys more than 300 days of sunshine a year and its coastline stretches out over 1,000km (621 miles). The best beaches are as follows. On the north coast, Cap Negro, 28km (17 miles) northeast of Tabarka, is sandy with rocks and is good for snorkelling. Cap Serrat, southwest of Bizerte, has a sandy beach with rocks, and Béchateur, 15km (9¹/₂ miles) west of Bizerte, has a sandy beach with rocks and little coves. For pure sand beaches on the north coast there is Plage de R'Mel and Rass Jebel, both east of Bizerte. On the Sahel coast the beaches are almost entirely sandy with no rocks, and the best are at Hammamet, Nabeul, Skanès, Sousse, and Port el-Kantaoui. The islands of Kerkennah and Jerba also have excellent safe sandy beaches.

Spas

Since Roman times the hot springs of northern Tunisia have been frequented for relaxation and for their health benefits. Modern treatment facilities and luxury hotels are now abundant as Tunisia has started to develop a well-being industry. Korbous, on Cap Bon, has seven springs with water ranging from 50°C to 60°C (122–140°F) and rich in minerals said to be effective in healing metabolic disorders and skin conditions, and in alleviating arthritis and rheumatism. Aïn Oktor, a few kilometres south of Korbous, is a cold mineral spring allegedly good for curing kidney stones. Jebel Oust, 30km (19 miles) south of Tunis, has springs (still with remains of the Roman marble floors) that soothe chronic rheumatic inflammations, arthritis and gout. At Hammam Bourguiba, 32km (20 miles) from Tabarka, is a spa resort with an excellent hotel. Its waters are recommended for alleviating respiratory disorders and curing allergies.

A *hammam* (public bath) entrance in Tunis' old médina

HAMMAMS (TURKISH BATHS)

One of the central tenets of Islam is cleanliness and Tunisians take particular care over their ablutions. Most modern houses have their own sanitation systems, but in older times and in médinas to this day, communal baths, known as *hammams*, were visited daily.

A *hammam* consists of a hot steam room where you sweat and can have a massage, and a cooling-off room normally where the changing room and lockers are. Most Tunisians still go to a *hammam* once a week because, once you have experienced the pleasure of a *hammam*, a conventional bath or shower just does not leave you feeling so clean. Going to a *hammam* is recommended at least once during your stay (although certainly not if you have sunburnt skin), as it is a very relaxing experience. After you have sweated profusely for a while in the steamroom, the masseur (or masseuse in a women's *hammam*) rubs you down all over with a coarse glove, which lifts off layers of old, dead skin. There are no sexual overtones to such massages and total nudity, which is not the norm, will be frowned upon, so don't strip off completely. Often, the same *hammam* is used by both men and women, although at different times of day, usually with men in the morning or evening and women in the afternoon. If you are insistent about having a his and hers *hammam*, the two hotels that offer this are the Hotel Palmariva at Jerba and the Hotel Chems el-Hanna at Sousse.

Shopping

Souvenir hunting is one of the most enjoyable parts of the holiday experience. The craft tradition is strong in Tunisia, with many excellent quality goods for cheap prices. Be prepared to haggle hard in the souks.

Bargaining

Bargaining is a way of life throughout the Arab world and, with the exception of food and medicine, it applies to most commercial transactions. In any bazaar, *souk* or souvenir shop, even when prices are marked, you can assume that there is latitude for a deal to be struck. And that is the important thing – striking a deal is not only a business transaction but also a means of social intercourse and communication. If you find bargaining awkward and stressful, it is best to avoid it altogether, paying the marked price, as this will still be less than the price you would pay at home.

When bargaining, it is important to stay calm and enjoy the experience over a couple of glasses of the requisite mint tea. If you are interested in buying only relatively cheap souvenirs, you won't lose out much if you don't bargain very hard. However, be more careful when you are spending more significant amounts on, say, a carpet or an antique. Do your homework and research the

prices at home first. There may not be a significant difference so, if you don't bargain, you may even end up spending more than you would at home.

There is no set price at which to start bargaining and no set rules. Some people start at one-third or half the price first quoted by the seller. One technique you can use is not to mention a figure at all until the seller has lowered the price considerably. Sometimes this can be as much as one-quarter of the original asking price. Do not quote a price unless you are genuinely interested in buying as this is considered very bad manners and will incur the wrath of the seller and of onlookers. Feigning lack of interest and walking away sometimes works, but you must not be too bothered whether you make the purchase or not, or whether you want the seller to lower the price.

Good souvenir buys

Caftans make excellent and original nightdresses, but when selecting a size allow for shrinkage of the cotton. Embroidered table napkins or tablecloths, cushion covers and tea towels all fit easily into a suitcase. Ceramics are fun but heavy and fragile, so you may have to restrict yourself to one large dish or a couple of mugs. Spices and herbs are tempting in the *souks*, but make sure they are packaged securely. Desert or sand roses (crystals of gypsum in the form of flowers) are unusual Saharan paperweights.

SOCOPA shops

The SOCOPA state-run handicraft shops (Maison de l'Artisanat Tunisien) have fixed prices for the goods they offer. This will give you an idea of costs before you bargain in the *souks* (*www.socopa.com. tn/index.php*).

OPENING HOURS

Most shops open: 8.30am–noon & 4–7pm in summer, 3–6pm in winter. The *souks* shut Fri pm and sometimes on Sun.

Souvenir shops line the streets in Tozeur

Pomegranates for sale at Houmt-Souk's market

The *souks*

Souks are Arab bazaars, and they are the best places for bargains when you go about purchasing your souvenirs.

Weekly markets

Outside the main towns, all shopping and indeed the entire economic life of rural communities, revolves round the weekly market. For outlying villages this is the event around which life is planned, the one time in the week when villagers not only make the purchases they need for the week, but also catch up on local gossip, see friends and even arrange marriages. Not surprisingly, these markets are highly colourful events. During your holiday you should seek out at least one, to drink in the

atmosphere even if not to buy. The best market in the whole country is at Nabeul, on Fridays.

Market days

Monday – Ain Draham, Beni Kheddache, El-Jem, Foum Tataouine, Houmt-Souk, Kairaouan, Kelibia, Makthar, Matmata
Tuesday – Béja, Bizerte, Kasserine, Kebili, Menzel Temime, Remla (Kerkennah)
Wednesday – Jendouba, Menzel Bourguiba, Nefta, Sbeïtla
Thursday – Douz, Gafsa, Hammamet, Le Kef, Menzel Bouzelfa, Siliana, Teboursouk
Friday – El-Faouar, El-Haouaria, Ghomrassen, Mahdia, Nabeul, Sfax, Tabarka, Testour, Zarzis
Saturday – Ben Gardane, Monastir
Sunday – Korba, Medenine, Metlaoui, Sousse, Tozeur, Remada.

What to buy
Carpets

These are probably the most expensive souvenirs available, and carpet-buying is not something to be entered into glibly. Always check for the ONAT stamp of authenticity on the underside,

---

CAFTANS

Caftans, known locally as *jellabas*, are the full-length, long-sleeved, cotton garments traditionally worn by both men and women. They tend to come in plain colours such as pale yellow or blue; you pay more for those with embroidery round the neck and chest.

which also has a brief description of the carpet's quality. Be sure that you are happy with your carpet – colours that look attractive in bright Tunisian sunlight may appear garish in duller Western climes.

Remember that duty and sales tax are payable on the full value, so it is essential to present the receipted invoice to customs authorities on arrival in your own country. Most good carpet shops will ship your goods to your home address for you.

Ceramics

While the Tunisian ceramics industry is centred on Nabeul and Guellala (Jerba), ceramics are found in shops all over the country. The shops in Nabeul have the lowest prices, with colourful styles, and plates and tiles are good buys here. While Nabeul ceramics show more Punic-Roman, Arab and Andalucian decorative styles, those from Guellala (Jerba) show Berber and Graeco-Roman influence.

Copper

In authentic town *souks* you can still watch sheet copper being hammered out into bowls, trays and *jardinières*, then chiselled with decorative patterns.

Jewellery

Coral and yellow amber necklaces are popular, especially in the Tabarka area. However, coral is endangered and protected. Any that you see on sale has probably been gathered illegally, killing the whole organism and stripping the reef. For once, it is better to buy the plastic version. All *souks* have a goldsmiths' quarter, but Houmt-Souk and Hara Kebira on Jerba are the traditional jewellery specialists, featuring the work of Jewish craftsmen. Good-luck charms invariably take the form of the Hand of Fatima or a fish, the two Tunisian symbols that ward off the evil eye.

Leather

Babouches, slippers with pointed, curled toes, make an excellent and inexpensive present. Unstuffed pouffes can also be fun. Fashion gear such as handbags, jackets and belts need to be carefully checked for the quality of their stitching and workmanship. Badly made items like these can fall apart

Wooden puppets, Sidi Bou Said street market

Highly decorative brass plates require the skills of a patient craftsman

after little use and turn out not be the bargains they seemed.

Perfume

Essence of rose, jasmine and lily of the valley are presented in little glass phials decorated with gold. Check that stoppers are in tightly.

Other items

There is a host of other attractive items that you can buy in Tunisia, including dolls in regional clothing, Sidi Bou Said birdcages in blue and white, lace and embroidery, *chechias* (red felt hats), fans of palm fronds impregnated with jasmine oil, turned wood objects like cigarette boxes, musical instruments and ancient weaponry like swords and daggers. Much embroidery work is enhanced with gold or silver thread.

You can choose clothing for yourself or for dolls dressed in various outfits, including traditional wedding dresses.

Tunisian crafts

The Tunisian traditional arts and crafts industry, which the government has worked to promote, caters mainly for the tourist industry. Different regions have their own specialities; Kairouan, for example, is famous for its carpets. These are made exclusively by women, and sold exclusively by men. The further south you go, the more strongly Berber the design of carpets becomes, with characteristic zigzags and lozenges in primary colours. Other purely female crafts are embroidery and lacemaking.

Nabeul is famous for its pottery. The pottery-making tradition here goes back to Roman times, and many of the ceramics made here are based on antique models. The white, green, blue and yellow, obtained from natural local materials, are the same as those used in Roman ceramic ware.

The most specifically Tunisian craft is the manufacture of highly ornate Sidi Bou Said white-and-blue birdcages, which are made in different sizes, but which are small replicas of buildings and of the *mashrabiyya* (carved latticework) windows of the traditional Arab house. They are, however, impossible to transport home except as hand luggage. These birdcages sit decoratively on the reception desks of many hotels, where they are used as the guests' post box.

Stuffed camels are cute, affordable and very portable, but don't expect them to survive the attentions of your child for too long. It's best to pay a little more and get ones that have a softer feel, especially if they are for younger children.

Ceramics for sale at Jerba

Entertainment

Most of the tourist resorts now have bars and nightclubs that cater specifically for tourists. Some Tunisians do frequent these places and drink alcohol despite their Muslim beliefs. Tunis has theatres and there are casinos in the main resorts.

BARS
Tunis and environs
Bar Jamaica. Great views of the city from this small bar on the 10th floor of the Hotel El-Hana International.
Avenue Habib Bourguiba.
El-Hana Brasserie. Ground floor in front of the El-Hana International. A people-watcher's paradise.
Avenue Habib Bourguiba.
Hammamet
Brauhaus. Great for German beer.
Opposite the médina in centre of town.
The British Pub (an original one).
Near the Hotel Bel Air in the Zone Touristique, Hammamet Sud.
Sousse
Rose & Crown. *Complex Touristique, Tej Marhaba Shopping Centre.*

CABARET
There are several possibilities in Tunis. Try **Mazar**, 11 Rue de Marseille, tel: (071) 355 077, **Flambo d'Or**, 8 Rue de Syrie, tel: (071) 831 539 or **Le Palais** at 8 Avenue de Carthage. All the large

beach hotels have their own cabarets and discos, while Hammamet has two independent nightclubs: the **Mexico**, near the Hammamet Sheraton Hotel; and the **Scheherazade Restaurant**, on Avenue des Nations Unies, where belly dancers, snake-charmers and fire-eaters perform.

CASINOS
Hammamet
Casino Cleopatre. *Hôtel Occidental, tel: (072) 226 633.*
Grand Casino de Hammamet. *Hôtel Azur, tel: (072) 261 777.*
Jerba
Pasino de Jerba. *Zone Touristique de Midoun, Jerba, tel: (075) 757 537.*
Sousse
Casino Caraibe. *Avenue du 7 Novembre, Sousse, tel: (073) 211 777.*

CINEMA
There is little or no incentive for the foreign visitor to go to the cinema in Tunisia. The staple diet is American

trash violence, Kung Fu and Indian boy-meets-girl sagas in which the lovers are thwarted by family and fate, but love triumphs over all in the end. The Hôtel Africa in Tunis sometimes shows more up-market French language films. Otherwise, Tunis has some 20 cinemas dotted about; to find out about the shows and their timings (usually 3pm, 6pm and 9pm) look in the French daily newspaper *La Presse*.

NIGHTCLUBS

There are nightclubs in the major tourist resorts and at most beach hotels. They vary in quality and most are of seasonal popularity.

Tunis and environs

Club 2001. *Hotel El Mechtel, tel: (071) 783 200.*
Jocker Club. *Hotel El Mana International, tel: (071) 331 144.*

Hammamet Sud

Calypso. *8050 Avenue Moncef Bey, tel: (072) 226 803.*
Cotton Club. *Avenue Moncef Bey, tel: (072) 248 855.*
Manhattan Club. *Avenue Moncef Bey, tel: (072) 226 226.*

Sousse

Maracana. *Avenue Taieb Mhiri, Tej Marhaba, Sousse, tel: (073) 299 800, fax: (073) 22815.*
Samara King Club. *Samara King Hôtel, Boulevard A. Kadhi, tel: (073) 226 699, fax: (073) 226 879.*

Theatre

Tunis has a **Théâtre Municipal** on Avenue Habib Bourguiba, with concerts of Arabic and Western classical music. The **Maison de la Culture Ibn Khaldoun** (*16 Rue Ibn Khaldoun*) also presents one-off performances by foreign touring companies.

Street musicians

Children

Children are adored in Tunisia as they are in all Mediterranean and Arab countries. The locals are always friendly towards families who come to their country for a holiday.

Babies

Most supplies for babies, such as powdered milk, baby food and branded toiletries, are available in tourist areas. Disposable nappies are also fairly easy to obtain, although larger sizes can be more difficult to find. If your baby is a fussy eater, it may be advisable to stock up on what he or she eats readily at home. If your baby requires any medication, get this at home and take it with you on holiday. Breastfeeding in public can cause offence, as Tunisians are fairly modest in this respect.

It is imperative that you keep your baby cool and hydrated in the summer heat. Car seats for babies and boosters need to be ordered when you book a hire car. If you need these, it is generally better to choose one of the international car-hire companies. Bring a pushchair or buggy as walking in heat can be difficult.

Highchairs are only rarely available in restaurants and you may have to sit your baby in the buggy at mealtimes. Changing areas are also few, so you may need to improvise, and this may also limit possibilities of trips any distance away from your base.

Beach

All children love the beach and smaller kids will be amused for hours playing in the sand with a bucket and spade. Older children will be interested in tanning themselves and will do so quite happily.

It is important to watch that your kids wear adequate sun protection and a sunhat during the middle of the day, to ward off sunburn and sunstroke. This is especially important for children with light and fair complexions.

The safest sandy beaches for young children are at Jerba, Kerkennah and Hammamet, and the hotel beaches at Nabeul (*see pp119, 76 and 58*). The rockier shoreline of the northern coast is less suitable for children. There are no dangerous currents offshore.

Food and drink

Traditional Tunisian food can be spicy and will not suit all children's tastes. However, Western-style cuisine is readily available in tourist resort areas, so that children will be able to eat familiar food. Most tourist restaurants offer smaller portions for children. Bear in mind that restaurants serving alcohol may also be smoky and less child-friendly.

Fun activities

Apart from the beach and the hotel pool, there are a few other options to keep your kids amused when on holiday. From some resorts, there are pirate ships that head out into the Mediterranean Sea. In Port el-Kantaoui (*see pp69–70*) there is even a yellow submarine that will take you under the waves. Ruins are often great places for kids to run about in and the Roman ruins, *ribats* and *ksour* of Tunisia are fuel to the mind of any imaginative child. Although some children find Roman ruins boring, others will run about pretending they are gladiators.

Matmata (*see pp128–33*) will capture the imagination of any *Star Wars* fan, young or old. The desert is the most exotic place to many kids. They may be disappointed that much of it is not what they expect, but when they

see the dunes they will be impressed. Younger children can run up and down the dunes. Older ones can go for a camel ride into the sunset, imagining that they are Berbers (*see pp126–7*) of the desert.

Hotels

While city hotels rarely cater for children, most of the larger beach hotels in all the resorts have playgrounds and children's pools. Many hotels will put a third bed in your room, which is obviously cheaper than booking an extra room. Very few hotel rooms have enough space for a fourth bed, so if you are touring and want to keep costs down, you may have to have two small children sleeping in the same bed.

Many beach hotels offer camel rides

Sport and leisure

Most large resort hotels are well equipped with sports facilities, some also offering gyms, exercise machines and aerobics sessions, as well as saunas and massages. Swimming pools are virtually standard and tennis courts and volleyball are very common.

Cycling

Many resort hotels rent out bicycles to guests. Ask at the reception desk.

Falconry

Falconry is practised at El-Haouaria, on Cap Bon, from March to June. In June, there is also the Festival d'Epervier, which is a celebration of falconry. The Club des Falconniers, also known as the Aquilaria, just outside El-Haouaria (on the road to the quarries) is open to visitors from 10am to 4pm daily and offers information on this pursuit.

Fishing

The best way to enjoy fishing in Tunisia is to arrange a trip out on a local fisherman's boat. Kerkennah is the best place for this. You'll find octopus fishing at Kerkennah, sponge fishing at Zarzis, and tuna fishing (from May to June) at Sidi Daoud, on Cap Bon. The diving school at Monastir can also arrange fishing trips, with rods and nets provided.

Football

Undoubtedly the national sport, football dominates Sunday afternoons all over the country. Tunisia is an improving nation in the world of soccer and the national team, the Carthage Eagles, qualified for the 2006

It's not advised to imitate the locals

4116 Midoun, Jerba, *tel: 659 0555, fax: 659 051; www.djerbagolf.com*
Port el-Kantaoui: El-Kantaoui Golf Club, Station Touristique d'el-Kantaoui, 4089, Kantaoui, Hammam Sousse, *tel: (073) 241 500, fax: (073) 241 755; www.kantaouigolfcourse.com*
Monastir: Monastir Golf, Route d'Oardinine, BP168-5000 Monastir, *tel: (073) 500 283, fax: (073) 500 285.*
Palm Links: between Sousse and Monastir, *tel: (073) 521 910, fax: (073) 521 913; www.golfflamingo.com*
Tabarka: Golf Montazah, Route Touristique, El-Morjanem, *tel: (078) 644 028; www.tabarkagolf.com*
Tunis: Golf de Carthage, Chotrana 2, 2036, La Soukra, *tel: (071) 765 919; www.golfcarthage.com*

Tennis is popular at the beach hotels

World Cup and won the African Nations Cup in 2004.

Golf

Because of its favourable climate, Tunisia is becoming increasingly popular as a golfing-holiday destination. The country has several golf courses, including:
Hammamet: Citrus Golf, BP132, 8050 Hammamet, *tel: (075) 226 500, fax: (075) 226 400; www.golfcitrus.com*
Yasmine Golf, BP61, Hammamet 8050, *tel: (072) 227 665, fax: (072) 226 772; www.golfyasmine.com*
Jerba: Jerba Golf, Zone Touristique,

Horseriding and racing

There are horses for hire on most tourist beaches and some of the large coastal hotels have stables attached.
Hammamet: Club Equestre, *tel: (075) 261 465.*
Tabarka: Hotel Golf Beach, *tel: (078) 673 002.*
For the less energetic there are race meetings every Sunday at the Ksar Said and Monastir racecourses.

Sand-yachting and land-yachting

Sand-yachting is practised on the dunes in the Kebili and Douz regions, while land-yachting (in a three-wheeled boat with a sail, rudder, seat and pedals) takes place on the great expanses of Chott el-Jerid. The Hotel el-Jerid, on the Kebili road 60km (37 miles) south of Tozeur, is the Tunisian land-yachting centre (*tel: (076) 450 488*).

Tennis

Most tennis is played on hotel courts, but if you fancy some serious opposition the main clubs in Tunis are the Belvedere Club in Parc du Belvedere, Avenue Taiet Mehin, and the Parc des Sports Club on Avenue Mohammed V. The Tunis Open Tennis Tournament takes place every year in March.

Walking

Tunisia has no mountains for the serious climber but it does offer good hill walking in the regions of Zaghouan, Kasserine (Jebel Chambi), Aïn Draham and Le Kef.

WATERSPORTS
Parascending

Increasing in popularity over recent years, this sport involves donning a parachute and being towed out to sea by a motorboat. As the boat builds up speed, the parachute fills with air and you are lifted up above the water, gradually descending again when the boat slows down.

Sailing

There are good marinas with excellent facilities at Port el-Kantaoui, Monastir, Sidi Bou Said and Tabarka. Mooring

fees are much cheaper here than in Europe, which makes Tunisia a popular sailing destination.

Scuba diving

Tabarka, in the north, is the best place in Tunisia for diving.

General information on diving in Tunisian waters is available from the Centre Nautique International de Tunisie, 22 Rue de Medine, 1001 Tunis, *tel: (071) 234 041*.

Diving schools offer professional instruction and training for an internationally recognised certificate.

Hammamet

Aquamarin Hammamet, Hotel Omar Khayem, Route Touristique, Mrezka, 8039 Hammamet, *tel: (072) 286 908*.

Monastir

Plongée & Loisirs de Monastir, Port de Plaisance, Cap Marina, Monastir, *tel/fax: (073) 462 509*.

Port el-Kantaoui

Club Sdanek Kantaoui, BP121, Port el-Kantaoui, 4089 Hammam Sousse, *tel: (073) 246 374; email: sdanek@planet.tn*

Tabarka

Aquamarin Tabarka, Hotel Abou Nawas Montazah, 8110 Tabarka, *tel: (072) 286 908, fax: (072) 287 547*.

Loisirs de Tabarka, Golf Beach Hotel, 8110 Tabarka, *tel: (071) 792 815* (Tunis office); *www.loisirsdetabarka.com*

Snorkelling

The best snorkelling is to be had along the north coast near Tabarka, where the rocky shoreline and coral banks attract a wider array of colourful sealife than the sandy beaches of the Sahel coast.

Swimming

Almost all the beach hotels in Tunisia's resorts have swimming pools in addition to their beaches. However, outdoor pools are rarely heated. Inland, it's hard to find a hotel with a pool and remember too that pools will only be filled and warm enough to swim in from June to September (night-time temperatures are still surprisingly low in spring and autumn).

Waterskiing and windsurfing

Most of the larger beach hotels have motorboats and can therefore offer their guests waterskiing. Most also hire out windsurfing boards and offer courses and onshore instruction if required.

The marina at Sidi Bou Said

Food and drink

Genuine Tunisian food is generally underrated, and it can be very good. By contrast, hotel food can be of a poor standard; it may also be quite bland, and mild flavours are typical because most hotel chefs believe that this is what Europeans prefer. To sample real Tunisian food, eat at a local restaurant. However, even this may not be of the highest quality. Few Tunisians can afford to eat out, so many restaurants rely on the tourist clientele and tailor their menus accordingly.

Tunisian cuisine

Although Tunisia is not renowned for its food, the best Tunisian cuisine, which combines the subtlety of French cooking and the spices of North Africa, can be delicious. The most characteristic national ingredient is *harissa*, a very hot spicy sauce made from dried ground red pimentos mixed with olive oil. *Harissa* is often served on the side of the plate, so it is optional, and rarely will a dish served to tourists, even in authentic Tunisian restaurants, be too fiery for European tastes. If you're concerned just ask for the dish to be prepared '*sans piquant*' and any *harissa* will omitted. Chicken and mutton are the commonest meats, with beef a rarity. Sweet peppers and green pimentos feature in most salads, with tomato, cucumber and black olives, usually swimming in olive oil.

Specialities to watch out for are:
baklava: flaky pastry saturated with honey and filled with chopped nuts.

brik: a crispy deep-fried triangle of filled filo pastry. Most common is *brik à l'oeuf*, filled with a soft, runny-yolked egg. Other fillings include spinach, tuna or anchovies.

Spices and pulses at Douz market

chakchouka: a vegetable stew with tomatoes, pimentos and onions, egg and perhaps some meat.

chorba tunisienne: a tomato soup sometimes thickened with pasta, and including onions and *harissa*.

doigt de Fatima: okra, a green finger-shaped vegetable, usually served stewed.

kaftaji: spicy fried meatballs containing chopped liver, peppers, courgettes and onions.

kamounia: cumin-flavoured slow-cooked meat or liver stew.

DRINKS

Tunisian wine

All Tunisian wine comes from the north around Tunis and on Cap Bon. Rosés are the most popular with Château Mornag Rosé and Gris de Tunisie the most common labels. For white wines try Blanc de Blanc or Muscat de Kelibia (not to be confused with the liqueur of the same name). Of the reds, Magon and Château Mornag are drinkable.

Beer

The only variety brewed in Tunisia is Celtia, a light continental-style lager, refreshing when served cold.

Spirits and liqueurs

There are four Tunisian spirits: *Boukha*, a clear white 'fire-water' spirit of distilled figs that can be drunk before or after a meal (try it with cola); *Thibarine* (originally made by the monks on the Thibar estate), a digestif, brown and sweet resembling cough mixture and drunk after a meal; Muscat Sec de *Kebilia*, a sweetish orange-coloured aperitif, good when chilled; and *Laghmi*, the fermented sap of the date palm. This is usually only tried once, even though it does have the reputation of being the drink of the Lotos-Eaters.

knef: lamb on the bone, seasoned with rosemary.

makhroud: semolina cake soaked in honey, with a date centre.

marcassin: wild boar, served with a strong dark sauce. It is available only in the winter hunting season and is the only pork eaten in Tunisia.

mechoui: grilled meat, usually lamb.

mechouia: grilled vegetables such as onions, peppers and tomatoes, mixed with olive oil and garnished with tuna and boiled egg.

merguez: solid mutton sausages strongly flavoured with red chillies.

mermez: mutton stew.

ojja: an egg dish with fried onions, peppers, tomatoes, *merguez* and *harissa* all scrambled together.

tajine: a lamb, egg and cheese dish, baked in a large tray, cut into square chunks and served cold in *casse-croutes*, though rarely in restaurants.

In the following listings the prices quoted are for a two-course meal for one, excluding alcohol, in an average Tunisian restaurant. Restaurants are divided into four categories

★   2 to 10 TD (Tunisian dinars)
★★   10 to 15 TD
★★★   15 to 25 TD
★★★★ 25 to 40 TD

The price of a bottle of Tunisian wine varies from 7 to 20 TD, according to the restaurant, and a beer can cost between 2 and 8 TD. A shot of spirits such as Boukha costs the same as a beer. Alcohol for consumption away from such premises as restaurants is sold only by special alcohol shops. They are always closed on Fridays and during the 30 days of Ramadan.

In the larger hotels and restaurants, a service charge of 10 or 12 per cent will automatically be added to your bill. In small establishments tipping is at your discretion.

There are some vegetarian restaurants springing up, but Tunisian cuisine is easy for vegetarians, with dishes such as *brik à l'oeuf*, vegetable couscous, and a large range of good fresh salads. Spinach, tomatoes, courgettes and aubergines figure large on most menus.

WHERE TO EAT
Tunis
Café Africa ★★★
Tunis' most upmarket café, air-conditioned and glassed-in.
Avenue Habib Bourguiba.
Chez Slah ★★
Offering French-style food and well-known for its desserts. Licensed.

14 Rue Pierre de Coubertin.
Tel: (071) 258 888.
Dar el-Jeld ★★★
Wonderfully restored médina town house, offering Tunisian cooking and music. Licensed. Smart dress. Closed Sun.
5 Rue Dar el-Jeld.
Tel: (071) 560 916,
www.dareljeld.tourism.tn
Dar Essaraya ★★★
Excellent Tunisian food served in a palatial, renovated médina house. Closed Sun.
6 Rue Ben Mahmoud.
Tel: (071) 560 310.
Gaston's ★★★★
A smart seafood restaurant, with a cheaper lunchtime set menu. Licensed.
73 Rue de Yugoslavie.
Tel: (071) 340 417.
La Mamma ★★
La Mamma has the best pizzas and pasta in Tunis. Licensed.
11 Rue de Marseille.
Tel: (071) 241 256.
La Petite Hutte ★★★★
Quiet, stylish French restaurant, highly regarded by locals.
102 Rue de Yugoslavie.
Tel: (071) 244 959.

Le Carthage ★★★
Behind the El-Hana Hotel, with a wide choice of Tunisian and Mediterranean dishes, and antiquarian décor.
10 Rue Ali Bach Hamba.
Tel: (071) 255 614.
Le Cosmos ★★★
A popular and lively bistro establishment. Licensed.
7 Rue Ibn Khaldoun.
Tel: (071) 241 610.
Le Palais ★★★
Licensed and with a nightclub atmosphere, serving excellent Tunisian food.
8 Avenue de Carthage.
Tel: (071) 256 320.
M'Rabet ★★★★
With an 'authentic' setting in the old médina above the Tourbet el-Bey café, M'Rabet is often block-booked by tour organisers. Licensed, with an accompanying show.
Souk el-Trouk.
Tel: (071) 261 729.
Restaurant Carcassone ★★★★
Clean, quiet restaurant that attracts locals and tourists. Friendly service, cheap delicious food.
8 Avenue de Carthage.
Tel: (071) 240 702.

TUNIS ENVIRONS

Gammarth

Restaurant Le Pêcheur ★★★
Excellent seafood lunches.
Baie des Singes.
Tel: (071) 749 955.

La Goulette

Monte Carlo ★★
One of the best local seafood restaurants and it is licensed.
Avenue Franklin Roosevelt.
Tel: (071) 735 338.

La Marsa

Café Saf Saf ★★
Set round a public well and taking its name from the white poplar trees in the main square.
Avenue 20 Mars.

Sidi Bou Said

Au Bon Vieux Temps ★★★
Excellent views and delicious food.
At the top of the village near Dar Zarrouk.
Tel: (071) 744 733.

Café des Nattes ★★
This is the café to stop at and have your refreshing cup of mint tea on a rush-matted seat.
Place Sidi Bou Said.

Café Sidi Chabaane ★
Café with one of the best views in Tunisia.
Rue el-Sidi Chabaane.

Dar Zarrouk Restaurant ★★★
An expensive and beautiful restaurant, set in palatial gardens with a panoramic terrace.
Below the Dar Said Hotel.
Tel: (071) 740 591.

THE NORTH

Aïn Draham

Beauséjour ★★
On the ground floor of the Hotel Beauséjour, Aïn Draham offers excellent ice cream served on the terrace.
Avenue Habib Bourguiba.
Tel: (078) 655 363.

Bizerte

Eden Restaurant ★★★
This is smartest of the corniche restaurants, and has an excellent choice of seafood dishes.
Corniche.
Tel/fax: (072) 439 023.

Le Petit Mousse ★★
The restaurant attached to the Petit Mousse Hotel, with an upstairs dining room. Grills and pizzas are served in the garden in summer.

Corniche.
Tel: (072) 432 185.

Tabarka

Café Andalous ★★
A lively café crammed with bric-à-brac.
Next door to the Hotel de France.

CAP BON AND HAMMAMET

El-Haouaria

La Daurade ★
Beside the entrance to the quarries (*see p56*), in a good cliff-top setting, and serving simple fish dishes. Crowded at lunchtimes, quieter in the evenings.
Seafront, near Les Grottes.
Tel: (072) 269 080.

Les Grottes ★★
Set well out of town, up on the cliff overlooking the quarries, this is El-Haouaria's newest restaurant. It is licensed and frequented by tour groups.
Rue des Grottes.
Tel: (072) 269 072.

Hammamet

Chez Achour ★★
Seafood specialities are served at this restaurant, which has a large and fragrant garden.

Licensed and quiet.
Rue Ali Belhaoune.
Tel: (072) 280 140.

Dar Lella ★★
Traditional Tunisian
fare in a domed dining
room, with a small
garden terrace.
Rue Patrice Lumumba.
Tel: (072) 280 871.

Sidi Slim ★★
Sidi Slim offers good
seafood and traditional
Tunisian dishes.
156 Avenue de Kowait.
Tel: (072) 279 124,
www.sidislim.com

Kelibia
Restaurant
El-Mansourah ★★
Wonderful views of
Kelibia castle. Terraces on
the rocky promontory.

TEA AND COFFEE

Mint tea is the national
drink, served heavily sugared
in a glass with a saucer and
tiny spoon. Milk in tea is
unheard of except in the
tourist hotels. Coffee is
served Turkish style, always
black and with three grades
of sweetness: very sweet,
medium-sweet or with just a
little sugar. The Arab style is
to have it flavoured with
cardamom. Western-style
cafés and restaurants also
have espresso machines.

Good fish and local wine.
El-Mansourah Plage.
Tel: (072) 295 169.

Nabeul
Au Bon Kif ★★
A good restaurant for fish.
On the corner of Avenue
Marbella and Avenue
Habib Thameur.
Tel: (072) 222 783.

Café Errachica ★
A great place for mint tea
served with pastries.
On the corner of Avenue
Habib Bourguiba and
Avenue Habib Thameur.

De l'Olivier ★★★
This is definitely the
classiest licensed
restaurant in town.
6 Avenue Hedi Chaker.
Tel: (072) 286 613.

THE SAHEL AND KAIROUAN

Iles Kerkennah
Restaurant La Sirène ★★
The best licensed
restaurant on the islands.
In Remla. Tel: (074)
481 118.

Kairouan
Café Halfaouine ★
This café has a terrace
to sit and watch the
médina.
Avenue Habib Bourguiba.

Sabra Restaurant ★
Clean with quick service.
Avenue de la République.
Tel: (077) 225 095.

Mahdia
Café Elkoucha ★
Chic café decorated in
a mix of Italian and
modern Tunisian with
tiled floors and
wonderful views of the
sunset. Italian-run, it
serves omelettes, pizza,
bruschetta and ice cream.
Cap d'Afrique.

Café Sidi Salem ★
Built into the side of a
cliff in a romantic spot
with sea views and two
nearby grottoes, this fun
café has terraces on
different levels and
offers sandwiches and
seafood.
Rue du Borj.

La Belle Vue
Restaurant ★★
Set away from the
médina with a shaded
terrace, this restaurant
serves attractively
presented fare such as
crevettes, dourade and
various beef dishes.
Avenue Farhat Hached.

L'Espadon
Restaurant ★★
A stylish licensed

restaurant with a fine beach terrace for outdoor eating in summer.
Beside the Sables d'Or Hotel. Tel: (073) 681 476.

Le Quai ★★

Le Quai is licensed and very busy, especially on Friday evenings. Seafood and meat dishes.
Avenue Farhat Hached. Tel: (073) 681 867.

Médina ★

Small, friendly restaurant next to the market with excellent fish couscous; popular with locals.
Place du 1er Mai.

Monastir

Bonheur ★

A cheap restaurant in the médina, serving basic food. Unlicensed.
Rue du 2 Mars.

Café El Bir ★

This café boasts an attractive courtyard with trees, and waiters in traditional brocaded waistcoats. There is an upstairs area for families and couples. It does snacks.
The médina.

Cap Grill★★

A top-quality seafood restaurant with a stylish location near the marina.

Marina Cap. Tel: (073) 462 136.

Le Chandelier ★★

Franco-Tunisian dishes are offered by this romantic venue where you can watch the boats from the window tables. The couscous and steak meals are recommended.
Marina Cap. Tel: (073) 462 232.

El-Ferik Restaurant ★★

Serving simple grilled fish or meat dishes on a pier off the corniche.
Corniche. Tel: (073) 460 717.

Port el-Kantaoui

Café Maure La Fontaine ★

In a pretty location by the fountain in the square, this whitewashed café has a light, airy feel and serves crêpes and light snacks. Friendly service with panache, good prices.
Rue des Palmiers, Place de la Marina.

Daurade ★★★

Expensive but with excellent fish dishes including seafood bisque, red mullet and lobster thermidor.
Marina. Tel: (073) 348 893.

La Méditerranée ★★★★

The best restaurant around the médina.
Marina. Tel: (073) 348 788.

La Nafoura ★

Simple, stylish pizzeria and patisserie serving light dishes, cream cakes and coffee. Relaxed, with lots of space for children to run around.
Les Maisons des Jardins.

Neptune VI ★★★

A floating restaurant offering fish specialities.
Marina. Tel: (073) 246 730.

Restaurant L'Escale ★★

Art-deco-style restaurant good for set lunches with fish, pasta and turkey dishes.
Rue des Jasmines.

Restaurant Les Orchidees ★★

Informal restaurant with an excellent selection of traditional Tunisian specialities such as *gargoulette d'agneau Berbère*, a spicy lamb dish. There is an upstairs terrace for outdoor eating.
Boulevard de l'Environment, Zitouna II.

Restaurant Nuova Marina ★★

This Italian restaurant

offers lasagne and pizzas as well as seafood risotto and veal cooked in Milanese style.
On the marina, set back from the quay.

Sfax
Bagdad ★★
Excellent Tunisian food is served here. Licensed.
63 Avenue Farhat Hached.
Tel: (074) 223 856.
La Sirène ★★
A great place for freshly cooked fish.
Marina. Tel: (074) 224 691.

Sousse
Le Gourmet ★★★★
Tunisian fish and lamb dishes cooked in earthenware pots in the oven are the specialities, Expensive, but worth it.
3 Rue Amilcar.
Tel: (073) 224 751.
Les Sportifs Restaurant ★★
With a good-value set menu and used to catering for tourists.
Avenue Habib Bourguiba.
Tel: (073) 224 756.
Le Surfin' ★★
Excellent selection of set menus with fresh fish and *tajine*. Children are charged half price.

Avenue Taieb Mehri/ corner of Rue Mongi Slim.
Restaurant Dodo ★★
In a corner of the médina close to the city walls, a quiet oasis offering simple dishes such as pizza, kebabs and *mechoui* (grilled meat).
Rue Hajra.
Restaurant La Fiesta ★★★
Good food, and it sometimes has belly dancers in the evening.
Rue Mongi Slim.
Tel: (073) 225 112.
Restaurant du Peuple ★
Tiny restaurant tucked in the shade of the médina walls with outside tables, offering a good range of couscous and *tajine* dishes.
Rue des Remparts.
Royal Sandwich ★
Fun place for eating chapattis, delicious unleavened bread, sliced, toasted or filled with fish such as tuna and spicy red *harissa* sauce. Friendly service and good prices.
Boulevard de la Corniche.

THE INTERIOR
Dougga/Tabersouk
Hotel Thugga Restaurant ★★
Your only option for lunch; rather bland.

Near main Tunis-to- Le Kef road.
Tel: (078) 465 713.

Douz
Restaurant Ali Baba ★★
Unexciting from the front, but a Bedouin tent behind. Good couscous.
Avenue du 7 Novembre.
Tel: (075) 470 978.

Gafsa
Restaurant Maamoun ★★
A good choice for reasonably priced food.
Avenue Taieb Mhiri.
Tel: (076) 224 441.
Semiramis ★★
The best hotel restaurant in town, part of the Gafsa Hotel. Serves stuffed squid and good Tunisian dishes.
Rue Ahmed Snoussi.
Tel: (076) 221 009.

Metlaoui
Hotel Restaurant Ennacim ★★
The safest food in Metlaoui is on offer here, the restaurant of the town's only hotel.
Route de Tozeur.
Tel: (076) 241 920.

Nefta

Café de la Corbeille ★
A rather touristy place,
but it has the best view.
Simple grilled food is
served in the evenings.
Near Hotel Mirage.
Tel: (076) 430 308.

Le Roi du Couscous ★★
This is a good place to go
for couscous dishes and
it is licensed.
Place de la République.

Tamerza

Tamerza Palace Hotel ★★★
The only restaurant
worth going to here, a
haven of cleanliness
and sophistication.
Route de Midès.
Tel: (076) 453 722.

Tozeur

Le Petit Prince ★★
The best restaurant in
Tozeur, with something
of a cult following.
Licensed and with an
attractive terrace.
Off Avenue Abou
el-Kacem Chabbi.
Tel: (076) 452 518.

JERBA AND THE SOUTH

Chenini

Relais Chenini ★
Simple eatery with basic

three-course lunches.
Old Chenini.
Tel: (075) 860 009.

Foum Tataouine

Hotel Sangho ★★
The restaurants in this
hotel are a real treat, with
good-quality pizzas,
Tunisian and French-
style food, served in
attractive surroundings.
Route de Chenini.
Tel: (075) 860 124.

Gabès

El-Mazar ★★
One of the most
expensive in Gabès, with
French food. Licensed.
39 Avenue Farhat
Hached.
Tel: (075) 272 065.

Tacapes Hotel ★★
The restaurant here
serves Tunisian and
international food. It is
licensed and popular.
Avenue Habib Bourguiba.
Tel: (075) 270 700.

Houmt-Souk

Blue Moon ★★
A quiet licensed
restaurant serving fish.
Try the *salade mechonia*
(a spicy mix of cold
vegetables). Eat in or
order take-aways.

Off Place Hédi Chaker.
Tel: (075) 650 559.

Dar Faiza ★★
Good value, with fish
and seafood specialities.
6 Avenue de la
République.
Tel: (075) 671 324.

Princesse de Haroun ★★★
The smartest restaurant
in town, with wonderful
lobster and squid dishes.
Marina.
Tel: (075) 650 488.

Ksar Haddada

Ksar Haddada ★★
Within the converted
ksar itself, serving tour
groups in its vaulted
chambers. Basic three-
course meals. Licensed.
5km (3 miles) north of
Ghomrassen.
Tel: (075) 869 605.

Matmata

Chez Abdoul ★★
Tunisian fare.
Centre of town.
Tel: (075) 230 189.

Zarzis

Amira Hotel ★★
The hotel's restaurant, on
the beach, is good value.
Zone Touristique.
Tel: (075) 680 188.

Hotels and accommodation

Tunisia is unusual in the Arab world for having had tourist-class hotels since the 1960s. The country offers a range of accommodation to suit all tastes and budgets, from basic and inexpensive to very luxurious.

The resort towns of Hammamet Nabeul, Sousse, Monastir and Jerba line the coast and are full of beach hotels specially designed for package-tour holidaymakers. Most hotel resort complexes are in *zone touristiques*, outside town or city centres. This preserves the atmosphere of historic town centres. The *zones touristiques* are only a short taxi ride from town centres.

Tunisia is now starting to offer traditional *dar* accommodation, similar to the Moroccan *riads*, and two of the first are Dar El Medina in Old Tunis and Dar Shiafa on Jerba, both of which opened in 2005.

RATES

Prices are seasonal everywhere except Kairouan, with cheaper rates between October and May, and top rates in the peak months of July and August. Service is generally added to the bill, and credit cards like MasterCard and Visa are accepted in all but the lowest and middle categories.

Hotels have three main price bands, which apply according to the season. The high season (*haute saison*) runs from July to mid-September; the mid-season (*moyenne saison*) from April to June; and the low season (*basse saison*) from November to March.

Prices at top-grade hotels range from 100 to 180 TD for a double room including breakfast, and they are equipped to a good international standard, with a minibar and television as standard. Top hotels also offer the usual range of executive services, from hairdressing and beauty salons to valets and conference facilities. During the low season, prices for a room in a top-grade hotel may be 30–60 per cent lower than during the high season.

Prices at mid-category beach hotels range from 60 to 100 TD for a double room including breakfast. Many resort hotels are so large that guests need never leave the site. They are totally self-contained, with sports facilities, souvenir shops, car hire agents and an excursions office on site. Large hotels aren't invariably ugly, high-rise blocks, however. Most of Tunisia's hotels are no taller than the palm trees that usually surround them. Two- to three-storey hotel or apartment blocks in well-landscaped gardens are also common.

Away from the beach resorts there are good-quality tourist hotels at the oases of Tozeur, Nefta and Douz. While they offer a similar level of service and facilities, they are generally cheaper than the beach hotels, with prices ranging from 50 to 90 TD for a double room including breakfast.

Inland, in non-resort towns such as Le Kef and Kasserine, the highest standard of hotel approximates to one- or two-star rating and costs from 40 to 50 TD. Facilities are limited, and the rooms are very basically furnished. Also, although the rooms have private bathrooms, the plumbing may not be of the highest standard.

Camping and hostels

Tunisia does not really offer camp sites in the European sense but there is one amazing sanitised campsite called Pansea Douar at Ksar Ghilane, where the beautiful tents have air conditioning and ensuite bathrooms, as part of the not-so-real-desert experience.

There are just a handful of simple hostels for students and backpackers, one in each of the main towns of Tunis, Sousse, Monastir and Nabeul.

Many of Tunisia's hotels are now built in traditional style, like this one in Nabeul

Converted *ghorfa* in the south

Tunis

In Tunis most good hotels are on or just off Avenue Habib Bourguiba, in the Ville Nouvelle (New Town). The two outstanding hotels here are the high-rise Hotel Africa Méridien and the El-Hana International, both on Avenue Habib Bourguiba. Mid-category hotels in Tunis are very few. In this range, the Hotel Maison Dorée is about the best, a relic of the French Protectorate and rather run down but the bathrooms have lots of hot water.

Tunis' cheaper hotels are to be found at the edge of the old médina, many of them round Place de la Victoire. Many of these are quite basic.

Tunis environs

If you do not want or need to stay in Tunis, you may find it preferable to stay in Sidi Bou Said, where accommodation is cheaper and more attractive. There is also a pleasant middle-range hotel, the Hotel Résidence Carthage, near Salammbô Tophet, which is open from April to October.

The north

In the north of the country facilities are limited except in Tabarka and Bizerte, where there are a handful of decent four-star hotels. Aïn Draham has a few former hunting lodges, and offers the closest accommodation to the Roman site of Bulla Regia.

Cap Bon

Hotels on this peninsula are limited as development here has not started. Cap Bon is still best suited to budget and independent travellers.

The coastal plain

Hammamet Sud has the greatest concentration of tourist hotels in the country. They are small, self-contained resort complexes and cater generally for those on package tours. Nabeul also has a few resort complexes.

Monastir and Sousse are the other major resorts of the east coast, with beach hotels in nearby Skanès and Port el-Kantaoui respectively. Skanès is somewhat blighted by noise from Monastir airport, but the beach is good. Port el-Kantaoui has a series of resort hotels built around a pleasant marina. It is solely a tourist town, with no centre as such.

Mahdia is a far more modest resort, with fewer hotels, although it has excellent beaches. Inland from the Sahel there is simple accommodation at El-Jem and slightly better accommodation at Kairouan, but nothing in the luxury class.

The interior

Apart from in the oasis towns, there is little tourist accommodation in the Tunisian interior, although rural tourism is beginning to develop. The oasis towns, however, are different. In Tamerza, the Tamerza Palace stands out as the only luxury hotel for miles around, while both Tozeur and Nefta offer several quality hotels. Kebili has one or two good standard hotels, but Douz is preferable, with several excellent places to stay, which are well designed and quite luxurious.

Jerba and the south

Many excellent self-contained hotels cluster along the northern shore of the Île de Jerba. Zarzis, on the mainland to the south of Jerba, is a small resort, quieter and with few hotels. The Berber hinterlands have a few basic hotels, in converted *ksour* and *ghorfas*. Most notable are in the *ksar* at Ksar Haddada and the exceptional Hotel Sangho, a four-star hotel outside Foum Tataouine. Matmata offers the ethnic experience of underground sleeping, though the plumbing may leave something to be desired.

Spacious swimming pool at Monastir's Sahara Beach Hotel

On business

Accommodation

The greatest number of business hotels are in Tunis and Sousse.

Banks

Although the Tunisian banking system has been restructured, it remains highly regulated. Moroccan banks operate under one of the toughest lending limits in the world: 7 per cent of net capital funds per borrower, compared with 25 per cent elsewhere. When setting up a company in Tunisia it is necessary to open a Tunisian bank account, where at least a quarter of the capital investment should be deposited. Tunisian banks are permitted to open foreign currency and convertible Dirham accounts to non-residents and companies.

Business hours

Banks: Monday to Friday, 8.30am–11.30am and 2.15–4.30pm in winter; Monday to Friday, 7.30am–2pm in summer and during Ramadan.
Business offices: Monday to Friday, 9am–noon and 3–6pm in winter; Monday to Friday, 8am–2.30pm in summer.
Government offices: Monday to Friday, 8.30am–noon and 2.30–6pm, and Saturday, 8.30am–1pm in winter; Monday to Saturday, 8am–2pm in summer.

Chambers of Commerce

Tunisian American Chamber of Commerce, 10 Avenue Mosbah Jarbou,
Rue 7116 El-Manar III, 2092 Tunis (*tel: +216 (71) 889 780, fax: +216 (71) 889 880, email: tacc@tacc.org.tn, www.tacc.org.tn*).
Tunisian British Chamber of Commerce & Industry, 23 Rue de Jérusalem, 1002 Tunis Belvedere (*tel: +216 (71) 802 284, fax: + 216 (71) 801 535, email: tbcci@gnet.tn*).

Conference facilities

Five-star hotels in Tunisia offer conference facilities.

Etiquette

On meeting business colleagues it is customary to shake hands and exchange business cards, which are usually in French, as this is the business language. Meetings and negotiations can be held in restaurants over lunch or dinner, even on weekends with high-level managers and company owners. If factory visits are involved, these should be within standard working hours. Some businesses close for half a day on Friday, and open on Saturday morning instead. Government and public-sector offices close on Fridays and on Saturday afternoons. Small gifts can be given to a Tunisian host, especially if you are invited to the home.

Exhibition organisers

Tunisie Voyages, Rue 8612 Imp N°4 Z.I. La Charguia 2035 Tunis. *Tel: +216 (71)*

205 500, fax: +216 (71) 205 186, email: dmc@tunisie-voyages.com
Visit Tunisia (head office), 68 Avenue du Koweit, 8050 Hammamet; branch office: Lotissement El-Jawhara number 4, Port el-Kantaoui. Tel: +216 (72) 280 860, fax: +216 (72) 283 120, email: visittn@gnet.tn

Media

The daily *La Presse* is the newspaper most widely read by businesspeople, as it has the largest business section. There is also the *Économiste Maghrabien*, a business weekly in French, and *Tunisia News*, a weekly in English, which also has a large business section.

Foreign companies

In order to do business in Tunisia, a foreign company must open a branch in the country.

To set up a branch you need to send a copy of the memorandum and articles of association and the company's main office address to the registrar of companies.

Government agencies

APIA (Agence de Promotion des Investissements Agricoles), 62 Rue Alain Savary, 1003 Tunis-El-Kadhra. *Tel: (071) 771 300, fax: (071) 796 453, email: Prom.Agri@apia.com.tn, www.Tunisie.com/APIA*
API (Agence de Promotion de l'Industrie), 63 Rue de Syrie, 1002 Tunis-Belvédère. *Tel: (071) 792 144, fax:*

(071) 782 482, email: api@api.com.tn, www.tunisianindustry.nat.tn
CEPEX (Centre de Promotion des Exportations), Centre Urbain Nord, Tunis-1080. *Tel: (071) 234 200, fax: (071) 230 297, email: info@cepex.nat.tn, www.cepex.nat.tn*

Investment

In 1994, an investment code was introduced that gives incentives including 35 per cent tax exemption on income reinvested in Tunisia, suspension of VAT on capital goods, and a 10 per cent reduction in customs duties on imported equipment that is not manufactured in Tunisia. Additional incentives are given to companies involved in export, regional development, agriculture, environment and technology.

Tax

Non-residents must pay Tunisian income tax at the normal rates.

Translation services

Most major hotels either offer a translation service or are able to recommend one.

Work permits

Foreign nationals working in Tunisia require a work permit, which is available from the Ministry of Social Affairs. Once you have obtained a work permit, you will also need to obtain a year-long residence permit from the Ministry of the Interior.

Practical guide

Arriving

Passports and visas

All visitors to Tunisia must have a valid full passport (British Visitor's Passports are not valid). European Union, United States, Canadian and Scandinavian passport-holders do not need a visa unless they intend to stay in Tunisia for more than three months. Australian, New Zealand and South African passport-holders need a visa, which can be obtained at the point of arrival in Tunisia. Other nationals need to obtain a visa from the Tunisian consulate in their country of residence before departure. Israeli nationals are not permitted to enter Tunisia, and if your passport has an Israeli stamp on it, Tunisian immigration officials may refuse you entry.

By air

Numerous airlines fly to Tunisia's six international airports, Tabarka, Jerba-Zarzis, Monastir, Sfax, Tozeur and Tunis-Carthage.

Carpet store in Toujane

Direct flights from the United Kingdom to Tunis are provided by Tunisair, the national Tunisian carrier (*www.tunisair.com*), and by GB Airways (*tel: 0870 850 9 850, www.gbairways.com*), a franchise of British Airways. Also, *flythomascook.com* has flights from Birimingham, Glasgow, London Gatwick and Manchester to Monastir.

Tunisair also provides direct flights from most of the European capitals, as do Air France and KLM.

As there are no direct flights from the United States, it is necessary to fly to Paris or London and catch an onward flight to Tunisia.

Fill in the arrivals card given to you on the airplane. This card will be checked at passport control on your arrival. Retain the departures portion, which will be collected by passport control on your departure.

Tunis-Carthage International Airport is near Lac Tunis, about 8km (5 miles) north of the city. Taxis are available from outside the airport terminal, and take about 15 minutes to reach the centre of Tunis, depending on traffic. You can also catch bus number 35 into the city centre.

By boat

Car ferries regularly sail between Marseille, Genoa and Trapani and La Goulette, the port for Tunis.

The crossing from Marseille, which takes 24 hours, is the most frequent. Contact the Compagnie Tunisienne de Navigation (CTN) for information and bookings (122 Rue de Yugoslavie, Tunis, *tel: (071) 242 775, www.ctn.com.tn*) or the CTN/SNCM (Societé Nationale Maritime Corse Méditerranée) at 47 Avenue Farhat Hached (*tel: (071) 338 222, fax: (071) 330 636*).

Arriving overland

Reaching Tunisia overland from the Algerian border is extremely difficult, though crossing the border into Tunisia from Libya has now become quite straightforward and quick. It is impossible to obtain a tourist visa for Algeria, but for Libya it has now become much easier, though you need to have obtained it in advance.

Camping

There are very few official campsites in Tunisia, and they tend to be very crowded in summer, when Tunisian students are on holiday. Tunisian campsite facilities are not to standards that you might expect in Europe. The better campsites are at Tozeur (Camping Les Beaux Rêves, *tel: (076) 451 242, fax: (076) 454 208*), Hammamet Sud (Samaris, *tel: (072) 226 353*), Nabeul (Camping Les Jasmins, Avenue Hedi Nouria, *tel: (072) 285 343*) and Ksar Ghilane (Camping Ghilane, *tel: (075) 470 750*). You can camp almost anywhere

unofficially as long as you have the landowner's permission.

Climate

If you want to swim in the sea or in unheated hotel pools, your visit to Tunisia must take place between April

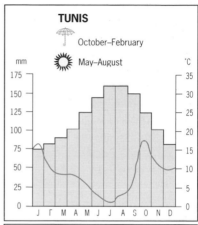

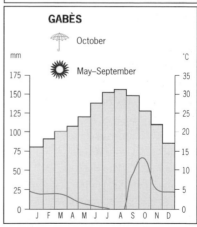

WEATHER CONVERSION CHART

25.4mm = 1 inch
°F = 1.8 × °C + 32

(preferably May) and October. Only the hardiest visitors will be able to brave the sea between November and March, and only then on the south coast round Jerba. Outdoor hotel pools are drained by this time anyway. For touring holidays, March, April and May are good months (although April can be rainy), as are October and November.

At all times of year the sun can be strong and the light dazzling, so always pack your sunglasses and use sunblock cream, even in winter. A pullover will be necessary in the evenings on the coast and especially inland, even in summer.

Conversion tables
See right.

Crime

As in most Muslim countries, crime rates are low compared to those we are used to in Western countries. However, theft is unfortunately on the increase, so keep your money and bag tightly closed when you are walking in crowded *médinas* and *souks*. Theft in your hotel is more likely to be committed by your fellow holidaymakers than the hotel staff.

Avoid unofficial guides. Many are conmen and before you know it your tour of the *souk* will end up in an unscrupulous back-street carpet shop, where you will be subjected to a heavy sales pitch. Your unofficial guide will get his commission if you buy anything at a hyped-up price.

CONVERSION TABLE

FROM	TO	MULTIPLY BY
Inches	Centimetres	2.54
Feet	Metres	0.3048
Yards	Metres	0.9144
Miles	Kilometres	1.6090
Acres	Hectares	0.4047
Gallons	Litres	4.5460
Ounces	Grams	28.35
Pounds	Grams	453.6
Pounds	Kilograms	0.4536
Tons	Tonnes	1.0160

To convert back, for example from centimetres to inches, divide by the number in the third column.

MEN'S SUITS

UK	36	38	40	42	44	46	48
Tunisia & Rest of Europe	46	48	50	52	54	56	58
USA	36	38	40	42	44	46	48

DRESS SIZES

UK	8	10	12	14	16	18
France	36	38	40	42	44	46
Italy	38	40	42	44	46	48
Tunisia & Rest of Europe	34	36	38	40	42	44
USA	6	8	10	12	14	16

MEN'S SHIRTS

UK	14	14.5	15	15.5	16	16.5	17
Tunisia & Rest of Europe	36	37	38	39/40	41	42	43
USA	14	14.5	15	15.5	16	16.5	17

MEN'S SHOES

UK	7	7.5	8.5	9.5	10.5	11
Tunisia & Rest of Europe	41	42	43	44	45	46
USA	8	8.5	9.5	10.5	11.5	12

WOMEN'S SHOES

UK	4.5	5	5.5	6	6.5	7
Tunisia & Rest of Europe	38	38	39	39	40	41
USA	6	6.5	7	7.5	8	8.5

24-hour Esso service station

impossible to avoid getting lost. Outside towns, roads are remarkably free of traffic and driving is easy.

Car hire

As hiring a car in Tunisia is very expensive, it is best to arrange this at home before your departure. The best car-hire deals can often be found on the Internet and most major car-hire companies have offices in Tunisia. You must be over 21 and have held a full licence for a year. Make sure you take out a Collision Damage Waiver (CDW) and before you set off check the spare tyre and make sure that the seat belts work. Child car seats are seldom available for hire in Tunisia, so take your own.

Emergency

In the event of an emergency contact the nearest police post. You will find police road checks at intervals of about 70km (45 miles). These are standard throughout Tunisia, and you will be asked for your driving papers.

Insurance

If you are bringing a car from Europe make sure that your insurance includes a Green Card that gives you cover for driving in Tunisia.

Petrol and diesel

Both four-star petrol and diesel are widely available in Tunisia. Unleaded petrol (*essence sans plomb*) is becoming more common. Fuel is still difficult to

Customs regulations

The duty-free allowance is 400 cigarettes, 2 litres (3½ pt) of wine, 1 litre (1¾ pt) of spirits and 60cc (2fl oz) of perfume.

Driving

Tarmacked roads in Tunisia are generally in good condition. Driving is on the right, and vehicles entering a roundabout have right of way over those already on it. The speed limit on the open road is 90kph (56mph). In town it is 50kph (31mph) and in built-up areas 40kph (25mph). All roadsigns are in both French and Arabic. They are clear and easy to read everywhere except Tunis, where it is almost

find in remoter regions, so fill up before you leave urban areas. In the most remote regions, especially in the south, fill your tank up whenever possible so as to reduce the risk of getting stranded.

Electricity
The standard 220-volt, 50-cycle AC is now used all over the country. Sockets take continental-style two-pin round-pin plugs.

Embassies and consulates
Australia: c/o Canada
Canada: 3 Rue du Sénégal, Tunis. *Tel: (071) 104 000, fax: (071) 104 190.*
New Zealand: c/o UK
Republic of Ireland: c/o UK
UK: British Embassy, Rue du Lac Windermere, Les Berges du Lac, Tunis. *Tel: (071) 108 700.* Emergency number (out of hours). *Tel: (098) 319 128.*
US: American Embassy, Les Berges du Lac, Tunis. *Tel: (071) 104 000, fax: (071) 104 190.*

Emergency telephone numbers
The national emergency telephone number is 197.
Ambulance: 491 313/284 808
Fire: 198
Police: 197
Doctors: it's best to ask at your hotel's reception desk.

Health and insurance
Up-to-date health advice can be obtained from your Thomas Cook

Ornate house detail

travel consultant. There are no mandatory vaccination requirements, and no vaccination recommendations other than to keep tetanus and polio immunisation up to date. As in every other part of the world, AIDS is present in Tunisia. Medical insurance is advisable for travel to Tunisia, as part of a travel insurance package.

Strict food and water hygiene is essential to avoid problems with diarrhoea. Make sure that food has been properly prepared; drink only boiled or bottled water, and remember that ice cubes are made with tap water.

Pharmacies are widespread and well stocked with most European medicines. Most pharmacists speak French,

although local tourist offices should be able to direct you to an English-speaking pharmacist.

Hitchhiking

Hitchhiking is possible in rural areas but is not recommended. In areas where bus services are infrequent, local people will pay the equivalent of a bus ticket for a ride in a private vehicle, and you will be expected to do the same. Never hitch-hike alone.

Internet access

Most major hotels offer access to the Internet. Internet cafés are springing up all over the country and you should easily find one in any of the major cities or resorts. Ask at your hotel. However, a broadband connection is still not standard, though facilities are improving all the time.

Maps

Tourist offices run by the ONTT (Office National de Tourisme Tunisien) will provide maps.

Measurements and sizes

See p176.

Media

Most tourist centres have European newspapers for sale the day after publication.

There are also three Tunisian dailies in French, two in Arabic and a weekly newspaper in English, *Tunisia News*.

Tunisia has two local television channels, one Arabic and one French, both of which have quite poor-quality programming. Most Tunisians watch the French television channel Antenne 2, which can be received all over the country. Television programme times are published in the three French dailies, *La Presse*, *L'Action* and *Le Temps*. Of the radio stations, Radio Monte Carlo is the most popular for music, while for news BBC World Service, broadcast from 5am till 11pm GMT on 15.07 MHz, is widely listened to.

Websites

Some general websites for visitors:
www.cometotunisia.co.uk
www.tourismtunisia.com
www.tunisiaonline.com

Money matters

The Tunisian dinar cannot be exchanged outside Tunisia. It is a soft currency, and exchange rates are fixed by the government. It is illegal to import or export dinar. Towards the end of your stay it is wise to shed as many of your dinar as possible, budgeting carefully.

Most small towns have banks at which you can cash traveller's cheques. Large hotels also cash traveller's cheques, at rates similar to, if not better than, those offered by banks. Credit cards are accepted in most large hotels and up-market restaurants, and Visa is the most widely accepted.

Languages

Although Arabic is Tunisia's official language, French is still widely spoken. Most common of all, however, is 'Frarabic', a haphazard mixture of the two, which most people speak in their own distinctive way, especially in the business community. Below is a selection of Arabic and French words and phrases:

English	French	Arabic
yes	oui	naam/ih
no	non	la
please	s'il vous plaît	birabee/min fadlik
thank you	merci	shókran
(very) good	(très) bon	béhi(yéssir)
bad	mauvais	mush béhi
go away	va t'en	imshee/barra
hello	bonjour	marhaba/aslama
goodbye	au revoir	bslémah
how much?	combien?	kadésh?
it's too much	c'est trop cher	yéssir
I would like	je voudrais	uhebb

Numbers

zero	zéro	sifr
one	un	wáhad
two	deux	tnéen
three	trois	tléta
four	quatre	árba
five	cinq	khámsa
ten	dix	áshera
twenty	vingt	ashréen
fifty	cinquante	khamséen
hundred	cent	mía
five hundred	cinq cents	khams mía
thousand	mille	alf

Street sign in Hammamet médina

to the left	à gauche	ala el-yassar
to the right	à droite	ala el-yameen
straight on	tout droit	tool
today	aujourd'hui	al yum
tomorrow	demain	ghodwa
yesterday	hier	ilbaareh
enough	ça suffit	izzi
bread	pain	khoubz
meat	viande	lahm
fish	poisson	huut
fruit	fruit	ghaláa
vegetables	légumes	khódra
water	de l'eau	meh
milk	du lait	haléeb
tea	thé	shay
coffee	café	kahwa
beer	bière	bíira
wine	vin	sharáb
red, white	rouge, blanc	ahmar, abiad
rosé	rosé	bordoukháli
salt	sel	milh
pepper	poivre	felfel akhal
sugar	sucre	súkar
the bill	l'addition	el-hisaab

Traveller's cheques in US dollars, sterling and euros are all accepted. Major hotels and some restaurants and shops in main tourist and commercial areas accept traveller's cheques in place of cash.

National holidays
Official holidays

1 January	New Year's Day
20 March	Independence Day
21 March	Youth Day
9 April	Martyrs' Day
1 May	International Labour Day
25 July	Republic Day
13 August	Women's Day
7 November	Day of Ben Ali's accession

Religious holidays

The main religious festival is Ramadan (*see p14*). The dates of religious festivals follow the lunar calendar and therefore move backwards by 11 days each year. Dates for the next three years are as follows:

	2007	2008	2009
Start of Ramadan	13 Sept	2 Sept	22 Aug
Aid El-Fitr	13 Oct	2 Oct	21 Sept
Aid Al-Adha (Festival of Sacrifice)	20 Dec		
Muslim New Year (Muharram)	20 Jan	9 Jan	29 Dec
Prophet's Birthday	31 Mar	20 Mar	9 Mar

Opening hours

Opening hours are not completely standard in Tunisia, but the bigger the shop the more likely it is to be open from 8am to noon and 3pm to 6pm. Restaurants tend to open from 12.30pm to 2.30pm for lunch and from 7.30pm to 9.30pm for dinner.

Museums and sites are open from Tuesday to Sunday, usually from 9am to noon and 2pm to 5.30pm in winter, and from 9am to noon and 3pm to 6.30pm in summer. The Bardo (*see pp28–9*) is the most notable exception to this rule.

Banks open Monday to Thursday from 8am to 11am, and 2pm to 4.15pm, and on Friday from 8am to 11am and 1.30pm to 3.15pm.

During Ramadan, working hours are generally shorter all round.

Photography

Photographic film is widely available in Tunisia, and at prices comparable to those in European countries. However, buy your film in a popular tourist destination rather than in remote towns, as there is likely to be a faster turnover of stock. If you buy your film before you leave for your holiday, it is imperative that you carry your film onboard with you and do not pack it in luggage to go in the hold. High-powered X-rays used at airports for scanning luggage will fog film. Carry-on luggage is X-rayed at lower powers that will not noticeably damage film even with repeated exposures.

Colonnade at Kairouan mosque

Because taking photographs in the strong midday sun results in pictures with harsh shadows and washed-out colours, the best times for photography are in the early morning and in the late afternoon.

Always ask before taking someone's picture, and never insist if they show signs of refusal. Street entertainers expect payment if you take a picture; they are, after all, putting on a professional show.

It is inadvisable to take photographs of official buildings or of official personnel (without permission). Pointing a camera at a police station, checkpoint, border crossing, bridge or communications tower, for example, can be misconstrued as spying, for which the penalty may be immediate arrest. Be particularly careful when taking photographs at Carthage and don't take photographs of the presidential palace. If you do, you will be reprimanded and your camera removed.

Places of worship

Visiting Christians may attend services at the Cathédrale de St Vincent de Paul on Avenue Habib Bourguiba, Tunis. Prayers at mosques may only be attended by Muslims.

Police

The Tunisian police service is modelled on the French system.

Taxis are the best way to get around

The Gendarmerie, whose officers are dressed in khaki, deals with state security, while those of the Sûreté (the ordinary police force) wear blue-grey uniforms. Officers of the Traffic Branch are recognisable by additional white caps and cuffs. Crimes and accidents should be reported to the Sûreté, whose officers usually speak good French. It is the Gendarmerie that carries out road checks in rural areas and frequently stops drivers as a security measure, particularly in the border regions. As a tourist you should have no problem with the Tunisian police, but you should always carry your driving licence, passport and car documents, which you will be asked to show if you are stopped.

Post offices

Tunisia's postal service, the PTT (Poste, Telephone, Telegraph), is efficient, with post offices throughout the country. Letters to Europe posted in one of the PTT's small, yellow post boxes usually arrive at their destination in 10 to 14 days. Post offices are open Monday to Friday from 7.30am to 1pm in summer, and from 8am to noon and 3pm to 6pm in winter, and on Saturdays from 8am to noon (shorter hours apply during Ramadan). Stamps are most easily bought at newsagents, postcard booths and souvenir shops, so that the only reason to go into a post office is to make a phone call from one of the booths (cheaper than calling from your hotel) or to send a telegram. The main post office in Tunis is in Rue Charles de Gaulle.

Public transport
By air
Tuninter, a subsidiary of Tunisair, the national airline, runs a limited number of internal flights (*www.tunisair.com*). Routes are from Tunis to Jerba, Sfax, Gafsa and Tozeur.

By bus and train
Tunisia's trains and buses provide a cheap and efficient transport network. However, tracking down departure information can take time and tickets must be bought at the relevant office before departure (*see p25*).

By *louage* and taxis
Within towns and cities taxis are by far the best way for foreigners to travel about (*see p25*). For longer distances between towns, the *louage*, a shared taxi for five people running on a fixed route for a fixed price, is fast and cheap, although it can take time to find the departure point in your town (*see p24*).

Student and youth travel
With a valid student card, students under the age of 32 may obtain reductions at sites and museums, and for journeys on internal flights and trains. A network of youth hostels is also open to all holders of an International Youth Hostel Card. The hostels are open 7am to 11pm. Contact: Association Tunisienne des Auberges de Jeunesse, 8 Rue d'Alger, 1000 Tunis, BP 320, 1015 Tunis RP. *Tel: (071) 353 277, email: ataj@planet.tn*

Sand dune at Douz

Sustainable tourism

Thomas Cook is a strong advocate of ethical and fairly traded tourism and believes that the travel experience should be as good for the places visited as it is for the people who visit them. That's why we firmly support The Travel Foundation, a charity that develops solutions to help improve and protect holiday destinations, their environment, traditions and culture. To find out what you can do to make a positive difference to the places you travel to and the people who live there, please visit *www.thetravelfoundation.org.uk*

Telephones

Mobile phone coverage (061 to 068 numbers) is about 90% in Tunisia, with two major local companies, Tunisia Télécom and Méditel, providing a service. The network runs on the European 900 Mhz GSM standard. So your mobile will work if your provider has a roaming agreement with one of the Tunisian providers. Roaming calls are expensive, and you can hire a local mobile phone for prolonged stays in the country or if you envisage making a lot of calls.

Calls from a PTT office are much cheaper than from hotels. You can either dial direct, feeding 1-dinar coins into the machine, or let a switchboard connect you, in which case you pay at the end of the call. For calls abroad from Tunisia, the international code is 00, followed by 1 for the USA, 44 for Britain, 33 for France and 37 for Germany. Local payphones take 100-millime coins and the local area codes are 071 for Tunis, 072 for the North and Cap Bon including Hammamet and Nabeul, 073 for Sousse to Mahdia, 074 for the Sfax region, 075 for the Gabès and Jerba regions, 076 for the Gafsa region, 077 for the Kairouan region and 078 for the Le Kef region. Dial 120 for business directory enquiries and 121 for private directory enquiries.

Time

Tunisia is one hour ahead of GMT, so in summer, when Britain is on British Summer Time, there is no time difference between London and Tunis.

Tipping

Waiters and taxi drivers expect a tip of 10 to 15 per cent, similar to customary practice in Western Europe.

Toilets

Public toilets do not exist in Tunisia (except in large railway stations and airports), so if you need one, find the nearest tourist restaurant or hotel. As toilet paper is not always provided, have plenty with you. Waste bins are frequently provided beside toilets to take the paper.

Tourist information

The government-run Office National de Tourisme Tunisien (*www.tourismtunisia.com*) promotes tourism. Most Tunisian towns have an ONTT office, or a smaller one often called a Syndicat d'Initiative.

Hammamet: Avenue de la République. *Tel: (072) 280 423.*

Jerba (Houmt Souk): Boulevard de l'Environment. *Tel: (075) 650 016.*

Monastir: ONTT, Rue de l'Indépendence. *Tel: (073) 461 960.*

Sousse: ONTT, 1 Avenue Habib Bourguiba. *Tel: (073) 225 157.*

Sfax: ONTT, Avenue Mohammed Khefecha. *Tel: (074) 211 040.*

Tunis: ONTT, 1 Avenue Mohammed V. *Tel: (071) 341 077.*

Travellers with disabilities

In Tunisia, facilities for travellers with disabilities are extremely limited. Wheelchair access in particular is rarely available, except in a few beach hotels like the El-Hana Beach and the Marhaba Beach in Sousse.

Palm trees on the beach at Jerba

Index

Acknowledgements

Thomas Cook wishes to thank the photographers, picture libraries and other organisations for the loan of the photographs reproduced in this book, to whom copyright in the photographs belongs.

ALAMY 93; FLICKR/Upyernoz 77, Manogamo 98; FOTOLIA/Jakezc 24, Rui Vale de Sousa 107; CONOR CAFFREY 6, 9, 14, 19, 28, 29, 36, 37a, 37b, 43, 58b, 71, 72, 74, 86a, 106a, 110, 111, 118a, 139, 172, 174, 178, 181, 186; MARY EVANS PICTURE LIBRARY 40. 41; PICTURES COLOUR LIBRARY 153; WIKIMEDIA COMMONS/BishkekRocks 39, 45, Douya 80; WORLD PICTURES/PHOTOSHOOT: 1, 31, 65, 141, 144, 147, 151, 156, 159, 188.

All remaining photographs are held in the AA PHOTO LIBRARY and were taken by STEVE DAY, apart from p116 ALEX KOUPRIANOFF.

Proofreading: JANET MACMILLAN for CAMBRIDGE PUBLISHING MANAGEMENT LTD

SEND YOUR THOUGHTS TO
BOOKS@THOMASCOOK.COM

We're committed to providing the very best up-to-date information in our travel guides and constantly strive to make them as useful as they can be. You can help us to improve future editions by letting us have your feedback. If you've made a wonderful discovery on your travels that we don't already feature, if you'd like to inform us about recent changes to anything that we do include, or if you simply want to let us know your thoughts about this guidebook and how we can make it even better – we'd love to hear from you.

Send us ideas, discoveries and recommendations today and then look out for your valuable input in the next edition of this title. And, as an extra 'thank you' from Thomas Cook Publishing, you'll be automatically entered into our exciting prize draw.

Emails to the above address, or letters to Travellers Project Editor, Thomas Cook Publishing, PO Box 227, Coningsby Road, Peterborough PE3 8SB, UK.

Please don't forget to let us know which title your feedback refers to!